EDUARDO MATOS MOCTEZUMA

The Great Temple of the Aztecs

Treasures of Tenochtitlan

Translated from the Spanish by Doris Heyden

with 158 illustrations, 23 in color

THAMES AND HUDSON

Half-title page: The head of the Coyolxauhqui
monolith, found in 1978. Compare ills. 14 and 133,
and color plate III.

Title page: The Aztecs attack the Spaniards
in Tenochtitlan, AD 1519. From the Lienzo de Tlaxcala.

© 1988 Thames and Hudson Ltd, London

First published in hardback in the United States of America in 1988 by
Thames and Hudson Inc., 500 Fifth Avenue, New York, New York 10110

First paperback edition 1994

Library of Congress Catalog Card Number 87-50201

ISBN 0-500-27752-4

Printed and bound in Germany

NEW ASPECTS OF ANTIQUITY

General Editor: COLIN RENFREW

Consulting Editor for the Americas: JEREMY A. SABLOFF

048381

CONTENTS

FOREWORD FROM THE EDITORS

If general readers were asked to name a Precolumbian civilization in the Americas, it is likely that the majority would select the Aztecs. Thanks to the popular historical writings of Prescott, and others, the exploits of Hernán Cortés' Spanish *conquistadores*, including the toppling of Motecuhzoma II and the great Aztec empire, have been etched in the public consciousness. Many people know of certain aspects of Aztec culture, such as their penchant for ritual sacrifice. The popularity of the recent bestselling novel *Aztec* by Gary Jennings is just one indicator of the hold that this ancient civilization still has on people's imaginations; and the Aztecs also play a large part in the more specialized archaeological literature, as the number of introductory books about them indicates.

How do we know so much about the Aztecs? The eyewitness account of the Spanish Conquest by Bernal Díaz del Castillo, and the descriptions of Aztec society by sixteenth-century writers such as the Franciscan friar Bernadino de Sahagún, have provided rich sources of information. Surviving Aztec literature and a variety of Spanish documents from the early post-Conquest occupation of Mexico have further deepened our appreciation. Unfortunately, there has not been a similar wealth of archaeological research and data. In particular, scholarly knowledge of Tenochtitlan, the great capital city of the Aztecs, is based mostly on non-archaeological sources. Given the highly centralized organization of the Aztec state, descriptions of Tenochtitlan have formed a key part of nearly all discussions. Yet because of the growth of present-day Mexico City – one of the largest urban centers in the world – directly on top of Tenochtitlan, archaeology has been forced until recently to play a limited role in research. Views of Aztec architecture, for example, were more readily available outside Tenochtitlan than inside the city.

A fortuitous discovery in 1978, however, has transformed the impact of archaeology on our knowledge of the Aztecs and we have been offered an unprecedented glimpse of remains at the very center of Tenochtitlan. The salvage work of Eduardo Matos Moctezuma and his associates, in the heart of Mexico City, has revealed a portion of the Great Temple (*Templo Mayor*) of the Aztecs, their most famous cult center. Not only has a large part of the structure been uncovered, but because of Matos' meticulous stratigraphic excavation its development through time can now be appreciated. In the pages that follow, Professor Matos discusses his discoveries and puts them in carefully described historical and cultural contexts. He offers, moreover, a stimulating interpretation of the role that the Great Temple played in integrating Aztec society.

Professor Matos' fieldwork brilliantly illustrates how archaeological research can illuminate a subject thought to be well understood from documentary knowledge. We feel strongly that the great potential of coordinated archaeological and historical work in the Americas will be given new support and meaning by this book, and especially by Professor Matos' ability to communicate the significance of the Great Temple Project to both students and the general public alike. As a result of this research, and its dissemination to the scholarly and popular worlds, new light has been cast on the growth of the best-known urban civilization in the Americas prior to the Spanish Conquest.

Jeremy A. Sabloff
Colin Renfew

INTRODUCTION

The purpose of this book is to introduce for an English-speaking audience the recent excavations of the Aztec Great Temple in Mexico City, and the light these have shed on Aztec civilization as a whole. The Aztecs – who knew themselves as the Mexica[1] but will, for convenience, be referred to in this book by the more widely known term applied to them since the nineteenth century – rose from humble beginnings to dominate much of what we now call central Mexico. They founded their capital, Tenochtitlan, in AD 1325, after many years spent wandering in search of a homeland. The site chosen was a previously uninhabited island near the western edge of Lake Texcoco, in the Valley of Mexico.

Spurred on by the belief that they were the chosen people of their patron deity, the war god Huitzilopochtli, they suffered long years of misery as vassals to other groups, such as the neighboring Tepanecs. By 1428, however, the Aztecs had achieved independence, and from their island-city they extended their authority during the fifteenth and early sixteenth centuries to create the largest empire ever seen in Precolumbian central America.

By this time Tenochtitlan was a magnificent, bustling city of perhaps a quarter of a million souls. Standing at its center was a huge ceremonial precinct, itself overshadowed by a Great Temple dedicated to Huitzilopochtli and the rain god Tlaloc. The Great Temple was the symbolic as well as physical center of the Aztec universe, and two centuries of imperial expansion had seen the edifice enlarged and rebuilt many times. But in 1521 this whole world was brought to an abrupt end by Spanish conquistadores under Hernán Cortés, with the support of rebellious Indian allies. The Aztecs witnessed the destruction of their temples and palaces, the Great Temple among them, and the imposition of

1

2 a new economic, social and religious order. The heart of the new Spanish metropolis was built directly over the site of the ceremonial precinct and the Great Temple. In time Mexico City, as it came to be known, grew to incorporate what had once been neighboring towns, such as Tenayuca, Coyoacan and Azcapotzalco.

Accompanying the conquistadores were Catholic priests, who – unlike their secular compatriots – set about learning the language, customs and beliefs of the Indians in order the better to understand the Aztec mind and thus ease the task of conversion to Christianity. During the sixteenth century a remarkable number of grammars, dictionaries, and histories of the Indians were produced by the clergy. Outstanding among them is the monumental, comprehensive, multi-volume work of Friar Bernardino de Sahagún, entitled *A General History of the Things of New Spain*. Also of great value today are the writings of Diego Durán, Toribio de Benavente (called by the Indians "Motolinía") and other friars, who tried to record as faithfully as possible what they saw and what they were told by native informants, so that their work would serve others in the spiritual conquest.[2]

These writings provide invaluable material for the student of prehistoric Mexico, and I make no apology for quoting extensively from them. They shed light in innumerable ways on the archaeological discoveries discussed in this book. Indeed, as will become readily apparent, the text that follows is an attempt not merely to describe the finds – the bare bones of archaeology – but to put flesh on them and to interpret them in the light of our current knowledge of Aztec belief and thought. For that the documents are essential.

Nevertheless, the archaeological work in Mexico City over several centuries forms the core of this volume, and it would be as well to begin with a brief account of my own career as an archaeologist, if only to indicate something of the variety of research that is going on in Mexico today and what lies behind the more spectacular discoveries detailed below.

While a student in the Mexican National School of Anthropology and History, I was fortunate to take part in excavations that began in Tlatelolco in 1960. Tlatelolco was Tenochtitlan's sister city, founded a little later than her neighbor, in AD 1337. Although work was carried out at Tlatelolco for a number of years, little has been published on these excavations. Shortly after this, I worked on a National Institute of Anthropology and History (INAH) project which examined the Classic-period city of Teotihuacan (AD 0–750), located to the north of

1 Model of a Chichimec temple in Tenayuca similar to the Great Temple of Tenochtitlan, crowned by the two shrines dedicated to Tlaloc and Huitzilopochtli.

2 An artist's impression of the Great Temple as it might appear if it were reconstructed in modern Mexico City.

Tenochtitlan-Tlatelolco. This project gave me an opportunity to study what had been one of the most powerful and influential cities of Mesoamerica.

After graduating, from 1966 to 1967 I helped direct excavations at another prehistoric city of great importance, Cholula, in the present-day state of Puebla. This project was under the overall direction of archaeologist Miguel Messmacher and aimed not only to excavate prehispanic remains, which covered a considerable time-depth, but also to undertake an interdisciplinary study of the entire area, including its history, language, and even the present socioeconomic situation.

When the Cholula Project finished I became Assistant Director of the Department of Prehispanic Monuments at INAH. Here I was active in the Tula Project at this predominantly Early Postclassic (AD 900–1200) Toltec city in the state of Hidalgo. Our main goal was to study the process of development in that region, also in interdisciplinary terms. Earlier work here had concentrated on the excavation of part of the ceremonial zone, but the full extent of the city was unknown. We had two concepts: the microarea and the macroarea. The microarea referred to the prehispanic city and its boundaries, as defined by archaeologist Juan Yadeum. The macroarea consisted of the area surrounding the city up to a radius of 15 kilometers; the objective was to do reconnaissance in order to locate other sites. Archaeologists Ana María Crespo and Guadalupe Mastache were in charge of this part of the project. At that time the University of Missouri began its own Tula Project under the direction of Richard Diehl, who has published the results in a companion volume in the New Aspects of Antiquity series.

In 1977 I was put in charge of the Great Temple Project (*Proyecto Templo Mayor*), which gave me a unique opportunity to penetrate into the heart of Tenochtitlan, now Mexico City. As early as 1794 Antonio de León y Gama had recognized that the excavation of the Great Temple site would be a very important project.[3] I excavated here over a period of five years, continuing the earlier work of archaeologists Manuel Gamio, Leopoldo Batres, Hugo Moedano and Ignacio Marquina. I was delighted to be named coordinator of the Great Temple Project, but realized that this was a challenge that could not be met by one person alone. Fortunately different departments of INAH became involved in the project, since from the outset it was recognized that Tenochtitlan had been the focus of the economic, social, political, and religious power of the Aztecs, and as broad a view as possible of the excavations would be needed.

7

Aware that our project was to be the first extensive excavation of this important site, we began with a thorough study of the historical documents referring to the Great Temple. In this way we were able to develop a theoretical framework and to anticipate at least some of the results of the excavations. But in many ways the excavations have told us much more than can be learned from history alone. For example, the wealth of materials found has clarified some aspects of the empire's economy and its relationship to the ideology of the Great Temple. The analysis and interpretation of these materials is a long and complicated task to which I am now dedicated, together with a number of specialists.

The idea of telling the story of Tenochtitlan and the Great Temple came from the General Editor of the New Aspects of Antiquity series, Colin Renfrew. I am indebted to him and also to Jeremy Sabloff for invaluable advice and encouragement. My gratitude is also due to the team at Thames and Hudson for their considerable help with the text, and their efforts generally during the production of this volume. I am especially indebted to my friend and colleague Doris Heyden who, with patience and dedication, translated the manuscript from Spanish into English and researched some of the material. To Debra Nagao, thanks for having carefully read and commented upon each chapter, and thanks also to my secretary Georgina Alonzo for her enthusiastic assistance. To all who have helped see the Great Temple of Tenochtitlan come to life once again, my deepest gratitude.

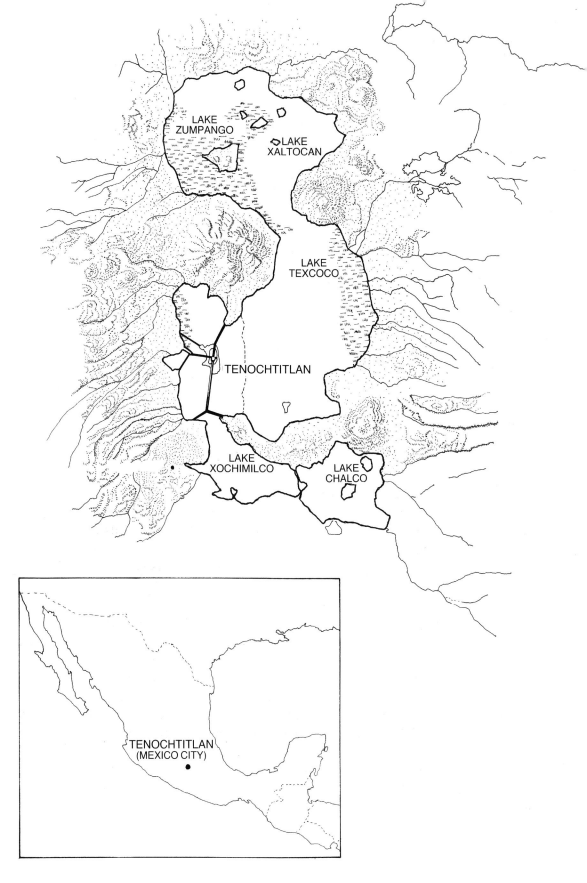

3 Map showing the location of Tenochtitlan on an island in Lake Texcoco: note the three causeways leading to the north, south, and west.

CHAPTER ONE

THE CITY OF MEXICO
PAST AND PRESENT

Mexico City is, today, one of the largest and most densely populated urban centers in the world. It covers roughly 1,300 square kilometers and in 1985 had about 17 million inhabitants. The Valley of Mexico, over much of which the city sprawls, has been the setting for human occupation since remote times, although the physical environment of long ago was vastly different from that of today.

The Valley nestles in a depression 2,500 meters above sea-level and is surrounded by lofty hills whose summits are inverted cones, thus revealing their volcanic ancestry. It was originally a basin, almost completely covered by a series of five lakes, the largest being Lake Texcoco. Today the minor lakes no longer exist, while Lake Texcoco has almost disappeared. But in ancient times they supplied important plant and animal foodstuffs for the local inhabitants, and were dotted with islands. The major island from the fourteenth century onwards was Tenochtitlan. In 1521 (the year of the Spanish conquest of Mexico), this little island, home of a great state and the capital of the Aztecs – who had been the rulers of central Mexico for about a century – covered 10 square kilometers[1] and had about 200,000 inhabitants.

The process of urbanization in central Mexico began around 600 BC, but there is evidence of human occupation thousands of years earlier, when the first bands of hunters and gatherers wandered through the Valley. At Tepexpan, not far from present-day Mexico City, hominid remains were found that Helmut de Terra has estimated to be 10,000 years old. One of the most curious finds was a fossil sacrum of the Camel family unearthed in Tequixquiac around 1870: this sacrum had been cut and perforated to give it the form of a wolf or coyote-head. Another interesting discovery of immature mammoth bones showing butchery marks was

3

made in Santa Izabel Iztapan; cutting implements associated with these bones were a scraper and an obsidian blade, and, particularly noteworthy, a flint projectile point found between two of the animal's ribs. Other mammoth bones, from a later discovery, also showed butchery marks: the cranium was found facing upwards and was undoubtedly placed this way to facilitate removal of the brain; some tools were associated with this mammoth. More recently, new finds, for example in Tlapacoya, seem to date the presence of man in the Valley of Mexico to around 20,000 years ago.

The growth of farming

Based on research by Richard MacNeish in the Tehuacan Valley in the state of Puebla, and on other complementary evidence, it is now accepted that agriculture developed in Mexico between about 7000 and 5000 BC. Plants such as maize, beans, avocado, chile, and squash were domesticated and people gradually came to depend more and more on farming. The resulting changes in the quality of life influenced the economy, social organization, and settlement patterns, and this is reflected in religion and art. As agricultural techniques developed, the early villages acquired a permanent character. Water and earth took on a fundamental importance and were deified by the community.

The development of ceramic technology aided the processing and storage of food. Also created from clay were small nude female figurines with marked sexual organs, probably forming part of a fertility cult. Such clay figurines have been found in the hills surrounding ancient Lake Texcoco since the beginning of the present century. When they first appeared it seemed that they differed from the more recent well-known Teotihuacan and Aztec figurines, and scholars attempted to classify them. Their research was advanced by the establishment in Mexico City in 1911 of the International School of American Ethnology and Archaeology, under the auspices of the governments of Mexico, the United States, France, and Prussia, as well as the Universities of Columbia, Harvard, and Pennsylvania. This new school was to prove of fundamental importance in the development of Mexican archaeology as a whole.

The first director of the School was Eduard Seler, and his successors included Franz Boas, George Engerrand, Alfred Tozzer, and Manuel

1 *General view of the Great Temple excavations, March 1981. The Coyolxauhqui Stone (color plate III) is visible in situ beneath scaffolding in the center of the picture.*

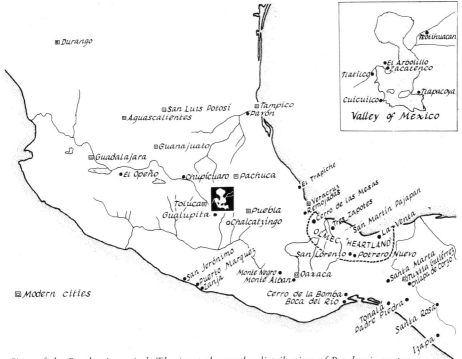

4 Sites of the Preclassic period. The inset shows the distribution of Preclassic centers in the Valley of Mexico.

Gamio. As a student at the school and under the influence of Seler and Boas, Gamio conducted the first stratigraphic excavation in the Valley of Mexico, between 1912 and 1913. Gordon Willey and Jeremy Sabloff, in their *History of American Archaeology*, describe this excavation as a "stratigraphic revolution." Carried out in Azcapotzalco, a suburb of Mexico City but once an independent town, it clarified the cultural evolution of the Valley of Mexico, which up to that time had caused confusion. Gamio established a stratigraphic chronological sequence: Aztec remains were found in the upper levels, with Teotihuacan sherds beneath, and the lowest level corresponded to what came to be termed the *Cultura de los Cerros* or "Hill Culture," now known as the Preclassic or Formative period (1500 BC–AD 150). During the Preclassic, self-sufficient villages depended economically on farming and fishing, and it is to this time that the early figurines are considered to belong.

Excavations by George C. Vaillant between 1928 and 1933 at El Arbolillo, Zacatenco, Ticoman, and other sites contributed more

4

II *The skull-rack altar, or "tzompantli," found to the north of the Great Temple. See also ills. 55–58.*

information about the Preclassic period. Both El Arbolillo – one of the oldest villages known in this area – and Zacatenco, lie in the northern part of the modern city and, like other early settlements, were situated to take advantage of the hillslopes that surrounded Lake Texcoco.

The rise of civilization

Around 1000 BC changes began to occur in Preclassic society. Sites like Tlatilco came under the influence of groups outside the Valley, including the Olmecs, who were developing an urban culture on the Gulf Coast of Mexico.

In the Valley itself, the first signs of urbanism, already fairly well advanced and thus possibly externally influenced, appeared at Cuicuilco. Excavations there by Byron Cummings in 1922, and again from 1924 to 1925, revealed part of a great stone circular temple base – about 150 meters in diameter – covered with mud plaster. Excavation of this structure was not easy because it was partially buried beneath lava from the small volcano called Xitle, located south of present-day Mexico City. The importance of Cummings' find was that it revealed the earliest ceremonial architecture in the area around Lake Texcoco. The construction dates from about 600 BC and indicates a social organization sufficiently stratified to control the labor necessary for the erection of such highly important religious structures. The discovery here of clay figurines representing the Old God of Fire is significant, as some of the volcanoes in the southern part of the Valley were apparently still active in Cuicuilco times. The same volcanoes that seem to have influenced beliefs and art may have been the cause of the eventual destruction and abandonment of Cuicuilco itself. A few years earlier Manual Gamio had excavated in nearby Copilco where he had also found very ancient remains beneath the lava. The presence of similar finds at Cuicuilco was not therefore surprising, although no monumental ceremonial architecture was discovered at Copilco.

In recent years INAH has excavated other buildings in the vicinity of Cuicuilco. These structures were square, and together with similar buildings excavated in Tlapacoya by Román Piña Chán, demonstrate architectural antecedents of what was to be the first truly great city in central Mexico, Teotihuacan. Tlapacoya (and Cuicuilco too) must have exercised some political and economic control over many villages.

Between 1976 and 1979 archaeologists from the National Autonomous University of Mexico, under María del Carmen Serra, carried out work in Terremote-Tlaltenco, a Preclassic-period village not far from Cuicuilco.

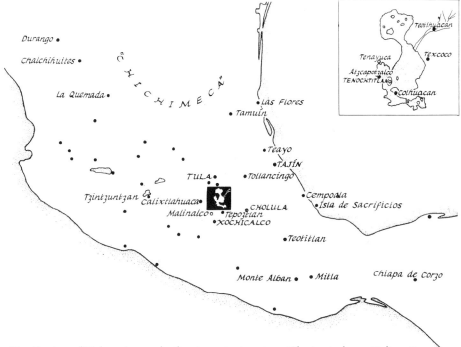

5 *Distribution of Toltec sites and other important centers. The inset shows Toltec sites in the Valley of Mexico.*

The inhabitants obtained fish, waterfowl, and other fauna from the nearby lake, and remains have been found of baskets, ropes, and nets, some of which were made from reeds which grew in the marshes.

Mesoamerican societies evolved rapidly after the Preclassic. Agriculture remained the basis of their economy, but economic expansion was also achieved through warfare and the exacting of tribute from conquered peoples. The state directed most activities, and power was wielded by an élite group. During the next two thousand years successive societies, such as the Teotihuacanos, Toltecs, and finally the Aztecs, left their mark on central Mexico, each one trying to control its immediate area as well as other parts of Mesoamerica.

Teotihuacan

Teotihuacan society evolved over hundreds of years (AD 0–750) and was characterized by monumental architecture, religious ceremonialism, a market system, long-distance trade, a ritual calendar, and highly developed arts. The city grew until it covered 20 square kilometers, with spacious avenues, religious and civil structures, plazas, and residential complexes. Its population is calculated to have been around 125,000. The presence of Teotihuacan culture traits in many regions of Mesoamerica attests to this society's powerful influence over other groups. But by around AD 750 the city had lost its hegemony, and parts of it were burned. This destruction may have been caused by the rebellion of outside groups against the centralized control exercised by Teotihuacan. People probably took advantage of weaknesses that by then were undermining the city's internal structure, a phenomenon to be repeated throughout the history of central Mexico.

Tula

The fall of Teotihuacan resulted in numerous cultural readjustments, and powerful new centers such as Cholula and Tula emerged. Initially two groups coexisted at Tula, creating what is known today as the Toltec culture, but eventually one group was ousted. The city flourished from AD 700 until its destruction in 1165, and grew to a substantial size, covering some 14 square kilometers, with residential complexes, ceremonial and civil edifices, and plazas. Eventually the Toltecs came to control much of central Mexico. They exacted tribute from conquered groups and it seems likely that at one time the Aztecs themselves were Toltec subjects. Whatever the truth of this, the chronicles record that the Aztecs migrated toward Tula in the twelfth century, arriving there in the year of its destruction, which must surely suggest that they had a hand in its downfall. Internal dissension among the Toltecs themselves also played a major part in the demise of their empire.

The Aztecs, as we have seen, founded their capital in the middle of Lake Texcoco in AD 1325. Tenochtitlan endured for nearly two hundred years before it was destroyed by the conquering Spaniards who used the stones of its temples and other buildings to create the colonial city from which today's Mexico City has grown.

The discovery of Aztec remains

It was not until the end of the eighteenth century that prehispanic Mexico again became a subject of interest. In 1790 work began in the Zocalo or main square of Mexico City to install water pipelines and to pave the plaza. During these operations various Aztec sculptures were unearthed, among them the famous Coatlicue – statue of the mother goddess – discovered on 13 August 1790, and the Sun (or Calendar) Stone, found on

6 Colossal atlantean figure of stone, one of four that surmount Pyramid B at the Toltec capital of Tula, Hidalgo. Each figure is made of four sections of stone and represents a warrior carrying a spear-thrower in one hand and a pouch for copal incense in the other. On the chest is worn the stylized butterfly emblem of the Toltecs. Ht 4.6 m.

17 December of the same year. Antonio de León y Gama gives us a contemporary account of these events in his famous book, *Historical and chronological description of the two stones found in the main square*:

I was . . . moved to write this in order to reveal to the literary world some of the vast knowledge that the Indians of this America possessed in arts and sciences in the time of their heathendom, so it will be known how falsely these enemies of our Spaniards are accused of being irrational or simple, in this way discrediting the glorious feats performed [by the Spaniards] in the conquest of these kingdoms. This written account and the pictures of the figures presented here will show that the people who made the original figures were superior artisans; although they had no knowledge of iron or steel, they carved statues of hard rock with great perfection in order to represent their feigned images, and created other architectural works, using as tools for these labors different stones that were even harder and more solid, instead of tempered chisels and steel-like axes.[2]

Writing at about the same time, the Dominican friar, Servando Teresa de Mier, lamented in his *Memorias*:

It is time that the venerable bishops learned a lesson from the impetuous judgment regarding these antiquities. The first Bishop of Mexico was inclined to believe that all the Indians' symbolic manuscripts were magic figures, witchcraft, and devils, and that it was his religious duty and that of the missionaries to exterminate them.[3]

In 1794 Teresa de Mier fell foul of the ecclesiastical authorities with a controversial sermon, and was moved to write:

When will these truly scandalous actions to destroy our monuments cease, which deprive us of the toil of our learned men and deny us knowledge of our antiquities, under the pretext of religion? The King, on the contrary, recently issued a Royal Order at the request of the Academy of History, not only that all the monuments of American antiquity be preserved but also inviting us to study them and to write about them. The Royal Order was communicated to us by the authority of the Royal Audience of Mexico.[4]

In 1803 the German explorer, Baron Alexander von Humboldt, visited Mexico. His observations were never equaled by any of the other nineteenth-century adventurers who penetrated the vast territories of America. Von Humboldt was particularly interested in archaeological sites and prehispanic monuments, and his experiences are related in his *Views of the mountain ranges and monuments of the indigenous peoples*

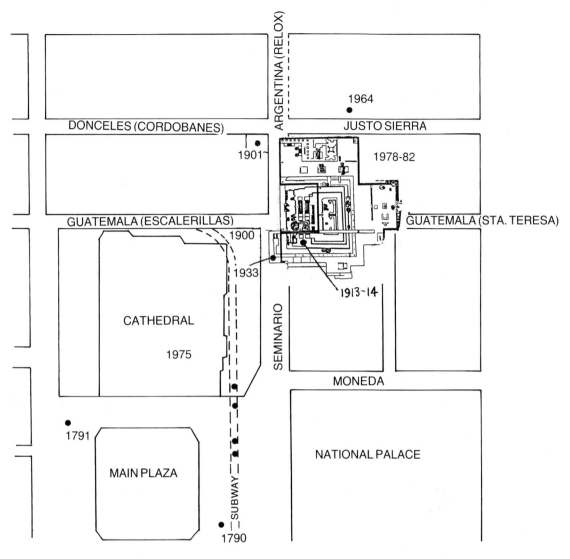

7 The central area of present-day Mexico City showing the site of the Great Temple of Tenochtitlan and streets in its immediate vicinity. The dates indicate years in which discoveries were made or excavations carried out, as follows: 1790 Coatlicue and Sun Stone; 1791 Tizoc Stone; 1900 excavations by Batres; 1901 P. Díaz; 1913–14 Gamio; 1933 Cuevas; 1964 Matos; 1967 subway excavations; 1975 Cathedral excavations; 1978–82 Great Temple Project.

of America.[5] Among the sculptures he discusses are those discovered in the Zocalo in 1790, including the Coatlicue stone.

By Von Humboldt's time, the Coatlicue sculpture had been moved to the University of Mexico on the orders of the Spanish Viceroy, who had had it measured, weighed, and drawn. Subsequently it had been buried in one of the halls of the University. Apparently this extraordinary step was taken because of the fears on the part of the clergy that such a "devilish

Famous Aztec finds of the eighteenth century

8 The great Calendar Stone features a solar diadem with an earth monster within at its center. The 20 day signs appear on the disk, but it is not a fully functioning calendar.

9 This sculpture of the goddess Coatlicue, "She of the Serpent Skirt," was reburied because of fears that it could provoke anarchistic ideas. The head has been severed from the body, and two serpents rise from the neck, meeting to form a face. She wears a necklace of human hearts and hands, with a pendant skull, and her skirt is a web of writhing snakes. Her hands and feet are tipped with monstrous claws. Ht 2.5 m.

idol" could provoke anarchistic ideas. The late eighteenth century was certainly a period of great religious unrest in Mexico. Von Humboldt takes up the story:

Count Revillagigedo, Viceroy, had this monument transferred to the University of Mexico, which he considered the most proper place to conserve one of the rarest remains of American antiquity. The professors, at that time Dominican priests, did not want to exhibit this idol to the Mexican youth so they buried it again in one of the halls of the building, at a depth of half a meter. Consequently, I would not have been able to examine it if Don Feliciano Marín, then Bishop of Monterrey, had not been going through Mexico on his way to his diocese and, listening to my pleas, asked the rector of the university to have it dug up.[6]

Many years passed before planned excavations in the center of Mexico City were undertaken, although when foundations were dug for buildings fortuitous discoveries occasionally shed light on prehispanic structures and sculptures. In 1825, a major find was the head of the goddess Coyolxauhqui sculptured in diorite. Peñafiel states that this was unearthed in the foundations of a house on Santa Teresa Street (now the continuation of Guatemala Street, east of the Zocalo). This house was the property of the Concepción Convent, and the piece was donated by the abbess to the National Museum.

In 1897 some carved stone pieces were found in the southwest corner of the Zocalo, at the intersection of the Merchant's Arcade (now the west side of the Zocalo) and Tlapaleros Street (now Sixteenth of September Street). One of these sculptures measures 1.65 meters long, 1.22 meters wide, and 0.68 meters high, and has on its sides armed warriors, carved in relief, with serpents above their heads. Another sculpture, 0.6 meters high, is carved on all four sides with representations of the four "suns," or cosmogonic ages.

Another discovery was made in 1901 during work directed by Porfirio Díaz, Jr, on the building destined to be the Ministry of Justice and Public Education, now the Subsecretariat of Culture, on the corner of Relox (Argentina) Street and Cordobanes (Donceles) Street. In the courtyard, part of a stairway running from east to west was found, together with a serpent head with a "4 Reed" glyph carved in relief, and a great stone sculpture in the form of an ocelot. The latter, called a *cuauhxicalli*, or "eagle vessel," is now in the Mexica Hall of the National Museum of Anthropology.

A year earlier Leopoldo Batres, Inspector of Monuments, had examined remains found beneath Escalerillas (now Guatemala) Street; he described

10 The ocelot or eagle vessel, discovered by Porfirio Díaz in 1901.

the objects in his *Archaeological explorations on Escalerillas Street.*[7] Batres mistakenly located the Great Temple beneath the Cathedral and gave it a southward orientation even though, as with most prehispanic temples, its façade actually faces west.

The archaeological investigations carried out in 1913 under the direction of Manuel Gamio, at the corner of Seminario and Santa Teresa Streets, are among the most important in the Zocalo area. Excavation became possible when a building was demolished, and as a result the southwest corner of the Great Temple of Tenochtitlan was discovered. Gamio included various specialists in this project, resulting in expert work on several different aspects of the finds. For instance, Hermann Beyer studied the banquette decorated with warriors, and Moisés Herrera classified the flora and fauna.

In 1933 the Direction of Archaeology department excavated at the corner of Guatemala and Seminario Streets, in the same block as the Cathedral, opposite the site where Gamio had worked. This investigation was led by the architect Emilio Cuevas; pits and trenches were dug throughout the entire area where some buildings had been demolished. Architectural features of particular interest found by Cuevas were a very elaborate balustrade and part of a stairway, perhaps belonging to the platform which supported the Great Temple in one of its latest building periods. Hugo Moedano and Elma Estrada Balmori explored this platform in 1948. It had been decorated with heads of snakes, a great serpent head, and a brazier, and all these sculptures were located in the middle of the south façade.

Other objects from the ancient city have continued to be unearthed in recent years. Some of these, reported by Eduardo Noguera, have come from the Republic of Cuba Street, at a place where a market was formerly located just south of the Zocalo. Others are from the excavations at Tlatelolco, about which only a minimum of information is available. Pablo Martínez del Río and Antonieta Espejo excavated at Tlatelolco in the 1940s, and their work was continued by Francisco González Rul in 1960 when the Nonoalco-Tlatelolco housing project began; Jorge Angulo has also made discoveries here.

In 1964 I excavated a decorated altar on Argentina Street, where a magnificent mural depicting the rain god Tlaloc was found on one of the sloping walls. In 1966 Eduardo Contreras discovered an important offering within the pyramidal structure of the Great Temple itself.

Work on the Mexico City subway began in the Zocalo area in 1966 and resulted in much new information about the ancient city. In 1973 the

7

IV

11, 12

11 The temple of Ehecatl-Quetzalcoatl, found in 1967 during excavations for the Pino Suarez metro station in Mexico City.

Salvage Archaeology department of INAH dug test-pits in the car-park of the Finance Ministry, located at one side of Guatemala Street. Some small altars were found here, but unfortunately they had been largely destroyed during the construction of the car-park. A year later, excavations in the Courtyard of Honor of the National Palace unearthed remains of some columns that probably belonged to Cortés' palace. A circular prehispanic altar was also discovered in the rear courtyard of the National Palace.

In 1975 the Department of Prehispanic Monuments started the Basin of Mexico Project. Its purpose was to control the constant and anarchic growth of the city, including the entire Federal District and adjoining areas, and to halt the destruction of archaeological remains. The metropolitan area was divided into four sections, consisting of a number of zones. Each section was under the supervision of a different team of specialists. In this way work was carried out at *Cerro de la Estrella* ("Hill of the Star"), Azcapotzalco, Xochimilco, Ecatepec, the Tepito district, and at the Metropolitan Cathedral. The Cathedral is of more direct interest than the other areas, the work here being organized by archaeologists under the supervision of Constanza Vega. Some Aztec buildings and ceramic remains were found beneath the Cathedral; the most interesting

12

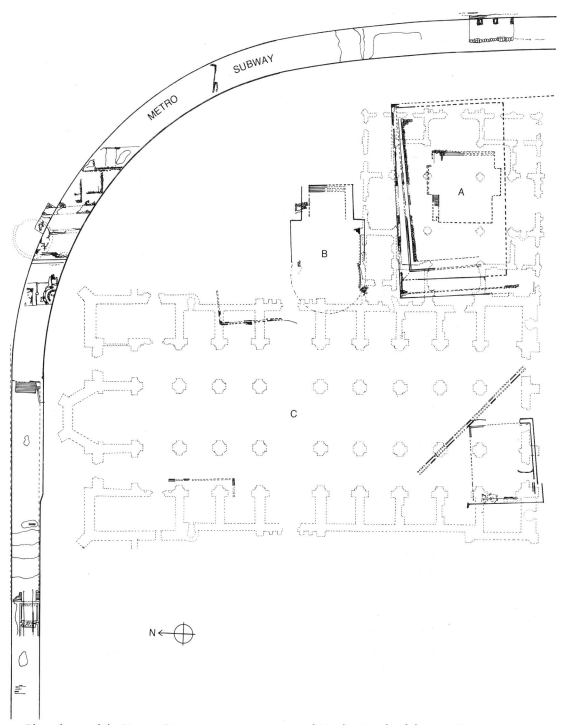

12 Plan of part of the Mexico City metro, seen curving round (A) the Temple of the Sun; (B) a shrine; (C) the Cathedral.

13 *The founding of Tenochtitlan, from the Codex Tovar.*

THE CITY OF MEXICO PAST AND PRESENT

discovery was part of a wall with a glyph in stone that may correspond to the Temple of the Sun.

The Museum of Tenochtitlan Project (1977) should also be mentioned. Its aim was to excavate the area where remains of the Great Temple had been found, and then to set up a museum at the site illustrating all aspects of the ancient city. This project was not, in fact, carried out, but was later changed into the Great Temple Project.

On 21 February 1978, workers from the Electric Light Company were digging at the corner of Guatemala and Argentina Streets in the very heart of Mexico City, when they discovered a large stone carved with a series of reliefs. They wisely decided to suspend work until the next day and contacted the Department of Salvage Archaeology of INAH. By 23 February it had been verified that the sculpture was a face in profile, with adornments on the head. Work continued for a further four days, revealing an enormous monolith 3.25 meters in diameter, with a representation of a decapitated and dismembered female nude carved in relief. This was a depiction of the goddess Coyolxauhqui who, according   *14*, III to Aztec myth, had been killed by her brother – the war-god Huitzilopochtli – following a desperate battle on Coatepec Hill.

An enormous mass of concrete beneath Mexico City covers many centuries of history. To penetrate this barrier and view the past we have to take advantage of opportunities provided by public or private works. Conservation and study of archaeological remains may help us to understand processes of cultural development not only in the past but also, perhaps, in the present, so that we may then look to the future.

The Coyolxauhqui Stone

14 A huge stone relief of Coyolxauhqui as a dismembered goddess, found in 1978 at the foot of the Great Temple stairway. The discovery sparked renewed interest in the remains of the Aztec sacred center and led to the Great Temple Project excavations.

III Professor Matos taking a cast of the Coyolxauhqui Stone in situ.

CHAPTER TWO

THE AZTECS
IN HISTORY

The archaeology of the Great Temple is closely interwoven with the history and myths of the Aztecs and one cannot be fully understood without reference to the other. Before examining the archaeology, therefore, we should look first at this historical background as it is revealed to us by sixteenth-century chroniclers.

History and myth suggest that, around AD 1000, the Aztecs left a place called Aztlan, their island homeland, and began to wander toward the Valley of Mexico. It is probable that at this time Aztlan formed one of the most distant outposts of the Toltec empire, with its capital at Tula. Although Aztlan's actual location has not been positively identified, it is thought to have lain to the north, in the area of the present-day states of Guanajuato, Jalisco and Michoacan. During the twelfth century, internal disagreements amongst the Toltecs, as related in their own histories, must have undermined the strength of their empire. This weakness, coupled with droughts suffered in the north, may have spurred Aztecs from all the seven districts (*barrios*)[1] of Aztlan to move south in an attempt to free themselves from the Toltec yoke. One of these *barrios* was that of the Huitznahua, "the Southerners," who were to play an important role in the pilgrimage.

Undoubtedly many features of the Aztec migration-story were taken from accounts of earlier peoples such as the Toltecs and Chichimecs, and were then incorporated by the Aztecs into their own histories. We shall now see what documentary evidence tells us about this journey.

IV *Detail of the banquette covered with reliefs from the interior of the precinct of the Eagle warriors. Stage V, c. AD 1480.*

15 Leaving Aztlan, from the Codex Boturini.

The journey from Aztlan

Friar Diego Durán described the migration as follows:

These people had left . . . some caves, seven in number, and the land they had inhabited, called Aztlan, which means Whiteness or the Place of Herons, and that is why these nations were called Aztec, which signifies "The People of Whiteness."[2]

Other chroniclers, such as Hernando Alvarado Tezozomoc and Domingo de San Antón Chimalpahin,[3] also refer to Aztlan. According to Tezozomoc:

Their dwelling place was Aztlan, and that is why they were called Aztecs; and the second name [of their dwelling place] was Chicomoztoc ("Seven Caves").[4]

The name of Chicomoztoc and also that of Teocolhuacan – important sites at the beginning of the migration – are taken from the histories of the Toltecs and Chichimecs. Chicomoztoc is mentioned both in the *Historia de la Nación Chichimeca* and the *Historia Tolteca-Chichimeca.*[5]

Some pictorial manuscripts represent Chicomoztoc as a cave inside a curved hill, and Colhuacan or Colhuacatepec means "Curved Hill."[6] Undoubtedly these symbols, the cave and the curved hill, as well as the number seven and other elements that the Aztecs adopted, were some of the ideas taken from histories of people who preceded them. As Paul Kirchhoff and Carlos Martinez Marin note,[5] the Aztecs must have considered the people to whom they were subject to be important.

15   The chroniclers tell us that the Aztecs left Aztlan under the orders of their war god, Huitzilopochtli, arriving eventually at Coatepec ("Serpent Hill") near Tula. Huitzilopochtli's relics were carried in a bundle by four

16   priestly leaders called *teomamaque*, or "god-bearers." Apparently it was not permissible to view the deity, and, according to Durán, even by the sixteenth century ". . . not one of these natives knows or has seen the form of this idol . . . "[7]

During their migration the Aztecs settled in different places, at times for a number of years, and in the course of their wanderings some important events occurred. One of these was their abandonment of Malinalxochitl, Huitzilopochtli's sister, who then founded the town of Malinalco, and whose son Copil was later defeated and killed by the war god.

Another major incident was the blasting of a great tree, which was seen as a warning to Huitzilopochtli's people to break away from the other

16 *Leaving Aztlan. Huitzilopochtli's relics were borne by four priestly leaders. Codex Boturini.*

Aztecs and to change their name: it was after this that they called themselves the Mexica. Huitzilopochtli was then to determine the destiny of his followers. Tezozomoc describes the god's promises:

We shall go to establish ourselves . . . and we shall conquer all the people in the universe . . . I will make you lords and kings of everything in every place in the world. And . . . you will receive an innumerable . . . number of vassals who will pay you tribute, who will give you countless and excellent precious stones, gold, feathers from the blue cotinga, the red flamingo, the *tzinitzcan* bird, all the precious feathers, and multicolor cacao, and cotton of many colors.[8]

The battle of Coatepec: history and myth

The Aztecs settled at Coatepec near Tula for a number of years. They built   17 dams and water channels to control a nearby river, thereby providing themselves with aquatic resources and irrigated fields for their crops. The Huitznahua, or "Southerners" – led by Huitzilopochtli's sister, Coyolxauhqui – thought that all the Aztecs should remain at Coatepec permanently. But this was not what Huitzilopochtli had planned for his people and it caused friction between his followers and the Huitznahua. In the struggle that followed, the former triumphed. This conflict has been interpreted as a battle between factions seeking to gain control over the entire group, but it can also be viewed as a symbolic representation of the destruction of the Toltec oppressor by the Huitzilopochtli-led Aztecs. The victory was later transformed into an important myth for the Aztecs: the birth of their patron god, Huitzilopochtli who, although in some accounts already in existence as a deified leader, in others was born at "Serpent Hill" in order to lead his people to victory.

17 *The arrival at Coatepec ("Serpent Hill") near Tula. Codex Tovar.*

Many myths are based on historical events important to a group, and the work of men then becomes the work of gods. Thus the human conflict at Coatepec became a battle between the gods, in this case Huitzilopochtli against Coyolxauhqui, with its accompanying symbolism. Sahagún, in his *History of the Things of New Spain*, has given an account of this event in mythical form, which can be summarized as follows:

9   On Coatepec Hill near Tula lived a woman named Coatlicue, "She of the Serpent Skirt," goddess of the earth, mother of the gods. One day, in a temple on the hill, Coatlicue was sweeping when a ball of precious feathers floated down toward her. The goddess picked this up and put it under her blouse, next to her breast; this action impregnated her. Coatlicue was the mother of four hundred
14   Southerners (the Huitznahua) and of Coyolxauhqui. When they found out that their mother was pregnant they asked her: "Who has done this to you? Who has made you pregnant? You have disgraced us, you have dishonored us." And Coyolxauhqui, the daughter, incited the others: "My brothers, our mother has caused us dishonor. We must kill her because she is perverse, she is with child. Who is responsible for the child she carries in her womb?"

Then the four hundred Southerners and their sister prepared for war and dressed themselves in battle array in order to kill Coatlicue. But the son within Coatlicue was Huitzilopochtli, god of war, and he comforted his mother with these words: "Do not be afraid, I know what I have to do."9

One of the Huitznahua, Cuicatlicac, whose brothers were doing all the plotting, revealed everything to Huitzilopochtli who was still in his mother's womb. Meanwhile the Huitznahua, led by Coyolxauhqui, marched in an armed column toward Coatepec Hill. But Cuicatlicac informed Huitzilopochtli of the route his brothers would be following and when they reached the summit of the hill, Huitzilopochtli was born. Sahagún takes up the story:

He was arrayed in his war dress,   *18*
his shield of eagle feathers,
his darts, his blue dart-thrower,
which is called the *xiuatlatl*,
the turquoise dart-thrower.
He painted his face
with diagonal stripes,
with the color called "child's paint" [offal].
On his head he placed fine feathers,
he put on his ear ornaments.
And one of his feet, the left one, was thin;
he wore a sandal covered with feathers,
and both legs and both arms
were painted blue.
And he who was called Tochancalqui
set fire to the serpent made of resinous wood
called the *xiuhcoatl*,
at Huitzilopochtli's command.
With this [Huitzilopochtli] attacked Coyolxauhqui,
he cut off her head,
which was left abandoned
on the slopes of Coatepetl.
The body of Coyolxauhqui
went rolling down
as it fell, dismembered,

18 Huitzilopochtli, arrayed in his war dress. Codex Tovar.

in different places fell her hands,
her legs, her body.
Then Huitzilopochtli rose up,
he pursued the four hundred Southerners,
he harassed them, he put them to flight
from the summit of Coatepetl, the mountain of the serpent . . . [10]

This myth is important for various reasons. On the one hand, it symbolizes the struggle of the sun, represented by Huitzilopochtli, against the deities of the night. Coyolxauhqui could represent the moon, while the four hundred Southerners may be the stars ("four hundred" means "innumerable" in ancient Mexican thought). The decapitation and dismemberment of the goddess is also linked to female sacrifice and to the moon which, as it waxes and wanes, evokes the idea of dismemberment and sacrifice. On the other hand, the fact that the Aztecs' principal god was created precisely in order to do battle may be a theological justification for the warlike character of Aztec society. Through aggression they could demand tribute – levied on conquered towns – in order to support the empire.

As we saw in Chapter 1, this myth became so important that it was re-
14 created in the Great Temple (the Coyolxauhqui monolith) when the city of Tenochtitlan was founded. This fits in with a cycle present in many myths, in which the historical event transformed into myth is in its turn made real through ritual.

The founding of Tenochtitlan

After the momentous events at Coatepec the Aztecs arrived at Tula around AD 1165, the year in which that city was destroyed, so it is likely that they played a part in its collapse. Later they continued toward the Valley of Mexico. The fact that they roamed from one place to another, probably being forcibly resettled, seems to indicate that all of central Mexico was organized into different chiefdoms already in control of the land, and because of this the Aztecs were obliged to become subject to the chieftain who dominated each region. This is what happened when they came to Colhuacan, governed by Achitometl; he allowed them to settle on the outlying lands of Tizapan and, in exchange, they had to pay tribute in the form of canoes and labor, fighting as mercenaries in Achitometl's wars of expansion.

At the same time the Aztecs tried to enhance their status by gaining permission to marry Colhuacan women, who were of Toltec descent. Achitometl even gave one of his own daughters to an Aztec leader. But the girl was sacrificed during one of their rituals, and this so incensed the Colhuacanos that they forced the Aztecs to flee and take refuge in the reeds and marshes of Lake Texcoco, on some swampy lands belonging to Tezozomoc, ruler of Azcapotzalco; since these bordered other chiefdoms and were undesirable islands, they had been left unoccupied. Thus was Tenochtitlan founded in AD 1325.

Here again myth is fused with historical fact. History relates that the Aztecs searched for a place to settle and found the swampy island controlled by Tezozomoc; he allowed them to live there in exchange for tribute and for mercenary labor in his wars against other chiefdoms. Myth, however, relates that this was the place chosen by their god Huitzilopochtli, and that here they would discover the signs promised by him. It is interesting to observe that the Aztecs borrowed from Toltec myth: these signs are almost the same as those discovered years before by the Toltecs when they reached the sacred city of Cholula. For the Aztecs, the signs were a white juniper tree at the foot of which would be found two great rocks; from these rocks flowed a spring of two colors, one stream red and the other stream blue. All the plants surrounding the spring were white and included reeds and rushes, and in the water the frogs, fish, and water snakes were all white.[11]

According to the chronicles, when the Aztec priests and elders found these signs they wept for joy and then spoke to their people:

We have discovered the place that was promised to us; now we have found consolation and relief for the tired Aztec people; now there is nothing more to desire. Console yourselves, sons and brothers, for what your god had promised you, we have discovered.[12]

That night the god spoke again to the priests, and told them that other signs were yet to be found:

You will remember how I commanded you to slay a nephew of mine named Copil, and how I ordered you to remove his heart.... The heart fell onto a stone, and from that heart sprouted a nopal cactus which is now so large and beautiful that an eagle makes his nest [there].... You will find [him] at all hours of the day, and around him you will see scattered many feathers – green, blue, red, yellow, and white – from the fine birds on which [he] feeds. And to this place ... I give the name Tenochtitlan.[13]

13, 19

43

19 Stone head of an eagle, from offering 78 within the Red Temple.

The next day the Aztecs, having heard the god's words, returned to the place where they had found the initial signs. Eventually they discovered the eagle upon the cactus. Durán describes this important moment:

Wandering from one part to another . . . they beheld the cactus and the eagle perched upon it. . . . And in its talons it held a handsome bird with precious and resplendent feathers. When they saw [the eagle] they humbled themselves before it. . . . The eagle greeted them humbly also, bowing his head low. . . . When they saw the reverence shown by the eagle, and knowing they had found what they desired, the men began to weep, . . . saying: "How is it that we deserve such happiness? . . . now we have obtained what we searched for, now we have found our city, our home. We give thanks to the Lord of Creation and to our god Huitzilopochtli."[14]

The Toltec symbolism of white plants and animals had helped the Aztecs find their sacred spot, but henceforward it was their own symbolism, the eagle on cactus, that would be elevated to the highest status. Not only did this symbol represent the heart of Copil who was defeated by his uncle Huitzilopochtli, but it also signified the triumph of the sun over its enemies. The eagle is thus a solar symbol, while Huitzilopochtli, as we have seen, is the sun itself.

Sacred and profane space

After the Aztecs had discovered their sacred site one of the priests urged them to give thanks to the god who had finally led them to their promised land and to erect a temple in his honor.[15] Construction commenced using reeds and straw, with swamp grass as a foundation. That night Huitzilopochtli spoke to the priest and advised him to divide the city into four *barrios*, with the temple at the center. Sacred space was thus separated from profane space.

20, 21

The sacred area or ceremonial precinct of Tenochtitlan came to consist of the Great Temple at the center with other temples and shrines eventually built around it. The whole complex was surrounded by a wall on all four sides. The sacred area could only be entered through the four gates which were oriented to the cardinal directions, as were the great causeways which led out of the city. One of these causeways went northwards to Tepeyac (now Villa de Guadalupe), another led to Iztapalapa in the south, and the third was the road to Tlacopan (Tacuba) in the west. The fourth road left the center of the city and went east to the lake which served as an aquatic highway. Cortés recorded that the causeway to Iztapalapa was as wide as two lances, so that eight horses could ride side by side along the entire length of it.[16]

Space outside the ceremonial precinct, that is, the *barrios* with houses of the nobles and those of the general population, remained profane space. Tenochtitlan was therefore planned symbolically, as can clearly be seen in the Codex Mendoza: here the eagle sits on the nopal cactus in the center of the illustration, in the spot where the Great Temple was to be erected. The four subdivisions indicating the major sections of the city radiate from the eagle, and these are oriented to the four quarters of the world. Beneath the eagle there are a shield and darts, and under these the name "Tenochtitlan."

20 Sacred space: the ceremonial precinct with the Great Temple in the center. Codex Matritense.

The Aztecs knew how to build on swamp land and the chroniclers describe the preparations made for laying a foundation for the city. According to Durán:

Little by little they made a terreplein and created space for their city; on top of the water they made a foundation with earth and stones that were thrown into the spaces between the stakes, in order to lay out their city on that surface.[17]

Initially the Temple and four main *barrios* – Moyotlan, Teopan, Atzacualco, and Cuepopan – were built.[18] Later, as the city grew, the number of *barrios* increased, and each one had its own god.

Twelve years after the founding of Tenochtitlan, a group of dissident Aztecs decided to settle elsewhere. In the year "1 House" (AD 1337) this group moved just north of Tenochtitlan to Xaltilolco, "On the Hillock of Sand," now known as Tlatelolco. From this time onward both cities, Tenochtitlan and Tlatelolco, underwent a parallel development, and they soon became rivals.

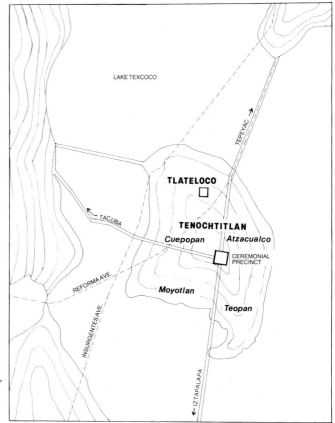

21 *Map showing the four main "barrios" of Tenochtitlan (in italic) and the causeways entering the city from the north, south, and west, all three leading to the ceremonial precinct. The dotted lines represent modern avenues.*

The Aztecs as vassals of the Tepanecs

Tenoch, one of the leaders of the Aztec migration, died around AD 1363, and so a new ruler (*tlatoani*, in Nahuatl "He who speaks") had to be elected. The Aztec advisers recommended that a member of the royal house of Colhuacan be sent to govern Tenochtitlan, since it was necessary for their ruler to have Toltec (Colhuacan) blood. As we have already seen, the Aztecs had cunningly intermarried with Colhuacan women and with these antecedents they were able to ask the Colhuacanos for Acamapichtli, son of one of their princesses, to rule Tenochtitlan.[19] Apparently Acamapichtli accepted his exalted position with humility, knowing that his people were vassals of the Tepanecs in Azcapotzalco. As soon as the Tepanec leader Tezozomoc heard about the new ruler, however, he and his council immediately decided to double the tribute to be paid by the Aztecs: up to that time it had consisted only of lake products and legumes, but from now on they were also to contribute junipers and willows, as well as rafts on which were to be planted vegetables such as maize, chile, beans, and squash. (It may be that the rafts referred to were actually *chinampas*, small artificial islands made of branches covered with mud dredged up from the lake bottom, today sometimes called "floating gardens," though in reality they do not float. The *chinampa* agriculture technique permits maximum utilization of a swamp environment, and is discussed below.)

Acamapichtli agreed to meet these demands. He governed Tenochtitlan for about thirty years and continued the city planning, but his main anxiety was his inability to free the Aztecs from Azcapotzalco domination. After his death he was succeeded by his son, Huitzilihuitl, even though it was Aztec custom to select the ruler's successor from the principal men of the royal house, rather than by kinship. During the accession ceremony the new *tlatoani* was formally reminded that the Aztecs were subjects of Azcapotzalco. Durán describes the election of Huitzilihuitl:

All the lords . . . went to the place where the elected king was [standing] and, choosing him from among the other youths and princes . . . surrounded him and took him to the royal palace, where they seated him and placed the diadem upon his head. And then they anointed his whole body with the pitch with which they also smeared the statue of their idol Huitzilopochtli. And placing the royal mantles upon him, one of the nobles spoke thus: "Courageous young man, our king and lord, do not be disheartened . . . we are under the protection of our god Huitzilopochtli, whose surrogate you are. You well know the fear with which we live and work . . . for we are subjects of Azcapotzalco. Tell yourself this and guard it in your memory, not so you will come to understand what is as yet unknown to you, but so you will acquire new courage."[20]

22 Acamapichtli, "Handful of Reeds," the first Aztec ruler.

26

The Aztecs then again attempted to use matrimonial alliances to avoid payment of excessive tribute. They asked for one of Tezozomoc's daughters to be Huitzilihuitl's wife, and from this union Chimalpopoca – their future sovereign – was born. Although the Aztecs tried to use Chimalpopoca to soften his grandfather's (Tezozomoc's) heart so that he would waive the tribute demands, only part of the tribute was rescinded.

The war of independence from the Tepanecs

The Aztecs had two major concerns while subordinate to Azcapotzalco. Firstly, they wanted to enlarge their main Temple and expand the cult of Huitzilopochtli; secondly, they wanted to free themselves from Tepanec domination. And so when Huitzilihuitl died in about AD 1417, Chimalpopoca was immediately named *tlatoani*, although still only a child. Without question the reason for this choice was to continue the policy of cordial relations with Azcapotzalco until the Aztecs could fight for their freedom; but the Tepanecs still refused them any concessions.

This was the state of affairs when the Aztecs decided to build an aqueduct to bring drinking water from Chapultepec to Tenochtitlan. It was a grandiose project with an elaborate construction of reeds, stakes, clay pipes, and mud, which had to cross the eastern reaches of the lake. Because of these difficulties, the aqueduct was constantly breaking and the Aztecs were forced to ask the Tepanecs for permission to build it of stone, which would have to be brought from the mainland. The Tepanec council not only refused this request, but Maxtla, son of Tezozomoc and lord of Coyoacan – a Tepanec chiefdom which lay southwest of Tenochtitlan – interfered with Aztec commerce and finally had the young Aztec ruler assassinated. Chimalpopoca's murder seems to have hastened the death of his grandfather Tezozomoc, by then an old man; he died in AD 1426 and Maxtla, who despised the Aztecs, ascended the throne of Azcapotzalco.

These events greatly strained relations between Tenochtitlan and Azcapotzalco. The tension escalated and finally led to the Aztec war of independence during the rule of Itzcoatl, son of Acamapichtli and uncle of Chimalpopoca, who was named *tlatoani* in 1427. Itzcoatl's election was due largely to his extensive military experience when, as a Tenochtitlan subject, he had participated in Azcapotzalco's wars of expansion. The Aztecs, led by Itzcoatl, finally defeated the Tepanecs in AD 1428. After a siege of 114 days, they and their allies from Tlatelolco, Texcoco, and Huexotzinco broke through the defenses of Azcapotzalco and entered the city, slaughtering many of their enemies. Durán tells of their triumph:

After their victory, like bloodthirsty, enraged dogs, consumed with fury, the Aztecs pursued [the enemy] who took refuge in the hills. There the Azcapotzalcos, prostrated on the ground, surrendered their weapons and promised they would give the Aztecs land, build their houses, till their fields, and become their perpetual subjects; they said they would provide stone, lime, and wood, as well as everything needed for their sustenance, such as maize, beans, *chía*, and chile, and all the vegetables and seeds that these people eat.[21]

And so, once again, the phenomenon that had existed in Mesoamerica for hundreds of years was repeated: tribute was imposed on a vanquished group, but now the roles were reversed.

The tribute the Aztecs imposed can be divided into three parts: tribute in labor, whereby women were forced into domestic service while men worked, for example, as masons or as supply-carriers in the Aztecs' wars; tribute in products, where the people of Azcapotzalco were obliged to give building materials to Tenochtitlan as well as agricultural products such as maize, beans, squash, chiles, and tomatoes; and thirdly, tribute in land. Lands were divided up so that the most fertile went to the *tlatoani*, with the rest destined for the *barrios*, the nobles, and the common men who had distinguished themselves in battle. In addition it was decreed that the Tepanecs were not allowed to choose their own ruler, but would be subject directly to the Aztec *tlatoani*.

The triumph over Azcapotzalco accelerated Aztec military expansion. The victory was first consolidated in the region of Lake Texcoco which had been a Tepanec stronghold; later other Tepanec chiefdoms, such as Coyoacan, were conquered. Soon Itzcoatl advanced on more distant regions, including northern Guerrero. In all of these campaigns he had the support of his allies, the Acolhuas of Texcoco and the people of Tlacopan. Together with Tenochtitlan, these two cities formed the Triple Alliance.

Itzcoatl died in 1440, having led the Aztecs to independence and founded what was to become the largest empire in Mesoamerica. He was succeeded by his nephew Motecuhzoma I, son of Huitzilihuitl, whose full name – Motecuhzoma Ilhuicamina – means "Angry Lord, Archer of the Sky." Motecuhzoma I continued the expansionist policies of his predecessor.

Aztec society

The way of life of the Aztecs is discussed in detail in Chapter 6 but, before turning to the archaeology of the Great Temple, a brief outline of the structure of Aztec society would be useful at this point.

Even before independence, Aztec society was highly stratified. The two most important groups were the lords and nobles (*pipiltin*) and the common people or workers (*macehualtin*). The nobles controlled the economic, political, social, and religious spheres. As we have seen, at the top of this group was the *tlatoani*, the supreme leader, elected from among the members of the royal houses. The sixteenth-century historian Alonso de Zorita has left a wealth of information about social stratification:

23, 24

When there were no brothers [to choose from] or when they were not prepared [to rule], [the council] elected the most capable relative of the deceased ruler; and if there was none, they chose another noble, but they never elected a *macehual*, which is a common man.[22]

The *tlatoani* had absolute authority, commanding both the ideology and the military might that sustained it. He imparted justice, received and redistributed tribute, and controlled vassals.

Another high rank was that of *tecuhtli*, a title usually awarded for outstanding military prowess. A *tecuhtli* could, like a man of noble birth (*pilli*), hold an office such as ambassador or tribute collector (*calpixqui*). The *calpulleque*, descendants of Aztec nobility, were the chiefs of the *barrios*: in general, the priests formed part of this class and were allowed to have private property, and the temples could also own land. Children of the noble class were trained in a special school, the *calmecac*. This school was the fundamental institution underpinning Aztec society, because it gave instruction in the entire ideological-religious system. Noble children were given specialized knowledge – such as religion and astronomy – to prepare them for their rank. Other privileges which Aztec nobles enjoyed included the following: they were not obliged to work the land; they could own private property; they held important public positions; they did not have to pay internal tribute; they had their own special courts of law to administer justice; they were allowed to use special insignia; they could have many wives or concubines.

23, 24 *Members of the Aztec working class* ("*macehualtin*") *included these porters* (left) *and fishermen* (right). *Codex Mendocino.*

Merchants played a particularly important economic role within Aztec society. Although they had to pay tribute to the *tlatoani*, they enjoyed privileges such as owning land or even their own armed forces. Furthermore, if one of them committed a felony, he was judged by a group of his merchant peers. These men also acted as spies; while on long-distance trading expeditions, they disguised themselves as locals and gathered information about other groups – such as defense measures and numbers of soldiers. As well as selling the products of their ruler and the state, merchants also traded their own goods in distant lands, thus monopolizing the market. We know that many merchants were from Tlatelolco, sister city to Tenochtitlan. Descriptions of Tlatelolco's famous market have been recorded by Bernal Díaz del Castillo and Hernán Cortés.

The majority of the city's population was made up of the working class (*macehualtin*), who were people from all the different *barrios*. They constituted the productive part of society, both in agriculture and craftsmanship. The working class included not only farmers and fishermen, but also potters, metalworkers, carpenters, stone-cutters, masons, and basket-makers. These people had to pay tribute to the *tlatoani* with their products and with personal service in public works required by the state, for example in the construction of temples, causeways, walls, drainage systems, and defensive barricades. Between twenty and one hundred men were organized into groups which rotated the rendering of these services according to *barrio*. The *macehualtin* were also soldiers, and upward social mobility was the reward for those who excelled in battle. *Macehualtin* youth attended a school called the *telpochcalli*, where they were trained for various occupations, and for warfare.

The farm laborers (*mayeque*), constituted another major group in society. They were permanent tenants who worked the nobles' land and to whom they were obliged to pay tribute. They also took part in war and they may have been able to acquire their own land if they were outstanding soldiers, but there is no clear information about this.

To be a slave, or *tlacotli*, was not an ascribed status. A person could become a slave for various reasons: nonpayment of internal tribute, failure to pay a creditor, or loss of bets in the ballgame (*tlachtli*), and failure to pay these debts. This ballgame was played with a rubber ball which had to be hit by the players' hips or shoulders. Only members of the ruling class were allowed to play the ballgame, perhaps because it took great skill and much time in training and the commoners had no time for this, nor did they have worldly goods such as jewels, fine textiles, or houses on which the players and observers bet. The game was an ancient one in Mesoamerica and had cosmic significance. Some interpretations claim that the ball court represented the sky, and the ball the sun crossing it, but there is no proof for this suggestion.

A thief or murderer became the slave of the person affected by his crime. A person could also sell himself or his child into slavery. In any of these cases, a slave could regain his freedom if he or his family bought his liberty, or if he escaped in the marketplace where he was being sold and managed to reach a temple or the palace. Similarly, a woman slave could better herself if she married the man whom she served. Owners had no ultimate rights over the lives of their slaves, and slavery never played a major role as a means of production in Aztec society.

Warfare, tribute, and the economy

Aztec society has at times been portrayed as revolving around the system of tribute payment: tribute collection ensured adequate productivity for the state. Tribute fell into two categories: internal and external. As we have seen, internal tribute was levied on the *macehualtin* who had to supply both goods and labor in public works and in military campaigns organized by the state.

External tribute was collected from non-Aztecs, victims of their military expansion. The Aztecs were not interested in owning these distant conquered territories, but rather wanted to harness the available manpower. Through the imposition of tribute, they could control the workforce and obtain products such as maize, beans, and fruit, and in this way warfare served a fundamental role in the acquisition of foreign goods.

V *Skeleton of a jaguar with a greenstone ball in its jaws, from Chamber II, part of the Stage IV Temple.*

VI *Conservation work being carried out on the polychrome "chacmool" statue found in front of Tlaloc's shrine at the top of the Stage II Temple. Compare ill. 35.*

V VI

Historian Friedrich Katz of the University of Chicago considers that tribute constituted almost the entire basis of the economy of the Triple Alliance (Tenochtitlan, Texcoco, and Tlacopan),[23] while anthropologist Pedro Carrasco of the University of New York states that, "most of the accumulation of goods in the royal store-houses of Mexico probably was obtained as tribute from subjugated provinces; therefore war was enormously important in sustaining and enlarging the economic basis of the great political centers."[24]

When the Spaniards arrived in Mexico in AD 1519, 371 towns were paying tribute to Tenochtitlan. As well as the agricultural products listed above, tribute could also be paid with cacao, honey, cotton, chile, and large baskets of maize flour, as well as loads of firewood and wood for building. There was also a great variety of manufactured products given as tribute, such as military uniforms, headdresses, banners, shields, insignias, cotton mantles, and women's blouses and skirts; paper, pottery, reed mats and other reed or straw objects, necklaces and other jewelry of precious and semi-precious stones, turquoise mosaic masks, featherwork and gold objects as well as commodities such as animal skins and marine shells. The Codex Mendoza mentions conquered towns and the tribute they were obliged to pay to Motecuhzoma II. Katz discusses the quantities, generally stated in *cargas*, collected in tribute:

25 *Eagle warrior depicted in the Lienzo de Tlaxcala.*

The Codex Mendoza states that a *carga* is approximately equivalent to 5,000 *fanegas* (about 144 liters). Based on this, Cook calculated that one *carga* (or load) contained about 600,000 kilos. He also figures that an average inhabitant of ancient Mexico consumed daily around 400 grams of maize, beans, and other edibles, which would add up to 146 kilos a year. If the eighty-eight *cargas* collected are converted into kilograms, the result is 52,800,000 kilos; if this is divided by the annual consumption per inhabitant, that is, 146 kilos, it can be concluded that this amount is sufficient to feed 361,641 persons a year.[25]

The tribute exacted must have been a tremendous burden for any conquered town. There were numerous attempts at rebellion against the Aztecs in order to escape payments, but these uprisings were violently crushed. Each *tlatoani* felt that one of his main duties was to extend the power and control of Tenochtitlan over other regions.

VII *Clay sculpture of an Eagle warrior found inside the precinct of the Eagle warriors. Stage V, c. AD 1480. Ht 1.9 m.*

26 *"Chinampas," or raised cultivation plots, in the vicinity of Xochimilco, Valley of Mexico.*

As already discussed, warfare was the only means of upward social mobility and the acquisition of land. An enlisted soldier who captured four enemies could become a government official or a captain in the army and be elevated to the rank of *tequihua*, which means "courageous warrior."[26] The most highly regarded warriors, however, were the Eagle or Jaguar knights, who were of noble birth and thus exempt from tribute payment.

Agriculture

Agriculture formed the other main component of the Aztec economy. Based on historical information, Teresa Rojas lists maize, chile, tomato, squash, and beans as the primary cultivated foodstuffs,[27] and amaranth was another important seed. By means of farming, hunting, and fishing, the Aztecs enjoyed a well-balanced diet.

Jeffrey Parsons[28] has carried out research in the southern part of the Valley of Mexico, once submerged beneath lakes, which was the *chinampa* region: this technique consisted of digging ditches or canals in swampy areas and leaving long raised plots or beds between the canals. On the edges of these plots a type of willow, *ahuexotl*, was planted; its roots became interwoven and thus ensured that the edges of the plots did not erode. Another way of making a *chinampa* was to cut out squares of turf and place them on top of one another – or at times on a "raft" of branches – until they were above water level, and then to plant on their surface. This *chinampa* farming technique, which seems to have been in use since Teotihuacan times (*c.* AD 500), permitted multiple harvests per year.[29]

Other agricultural techniques included the control of water supplies including springs, and the use of irrigation canals and terracing. Methods of intensification in Mesoamerica have been studied by a number of authors, such as Robert West, Pedro Armillas, Angel Palerm,[30] Eric Wolf, and Teresa Rojas. According to Rojas, the three agricultural implements most commonly employed were the *uitzoctli* or digging stick, also known as the *coa*; the *uictli* or bladed *coa*; and the *uictli axoquen*, the *coa* with a zoomorphic handle. The *uitzoctli* was made of oak and had a very sharp point that was fire-hardened. The *uictli* was also of oak, but its end flared out to form a triangular point, and the *uictli axoquen* was formed by two pieces that were tied together with a handle in the form of an animal head at the top.[31] There were also other implements used in the different stages of planting, harvesting, and food manufacture. These included stone or copper axes with wooden handles, and grinding stones used for crushing kernels of maize into flour.

27 An Aztec wielding a digging stick. Codex Osuna.

Many dishes, such as tortillas, tamales, and *atole* gruel, were derived from maize, and even today these are an essential part of the daily diet. The chroniclers describe both the nutritional and religious values of these foods. For example, Sahagún[32] describes the twenty-day feast called Huauhquiltamalqualiztli, "The eating of tamales with amaranth leaves" in honor of the Fire God, when tamales made of maize dough wrapped in amaranth leaves were consumed. People took tamales to the temple, offered them to the fire in the home, and placed them where their dead lay buried. Another feast, celebrated every eight years, was Atamalaqualiztli, "The eating of water tamales." This was a period of fasting when for eight days people ate only unsalted tamales, without chile or greens, and drank water.[33] Durán records the feast called Etzalcualiztli, "The eating of corn cooked with beans:"

Etzalcualiztli . . . means "day on which *etzalli* is allowed to be eaten". . . . It is a sort of bean stew containing whole kernels of corn. It is considered very tasty, so coveted, so greatly desired, that it is small wonder it had its own special day and feast on which it was honored.[34]

The preceding background on Aztec history, social stratification, and economy is crucial for an understanding of the culture as a whole. Agriculture, combined with warfare and the tribute it entailed, served as the foundation on which rested the entire economy. This is clearly manifested in the principal cult center of the Aztecs, the Great Temple of Tenochtitlan. Here, in the symbolism of the supreme ceremonial focus of the empire, we shall see the complex interweaving of strands of history and myth, and of economic, political, and religious concerns.

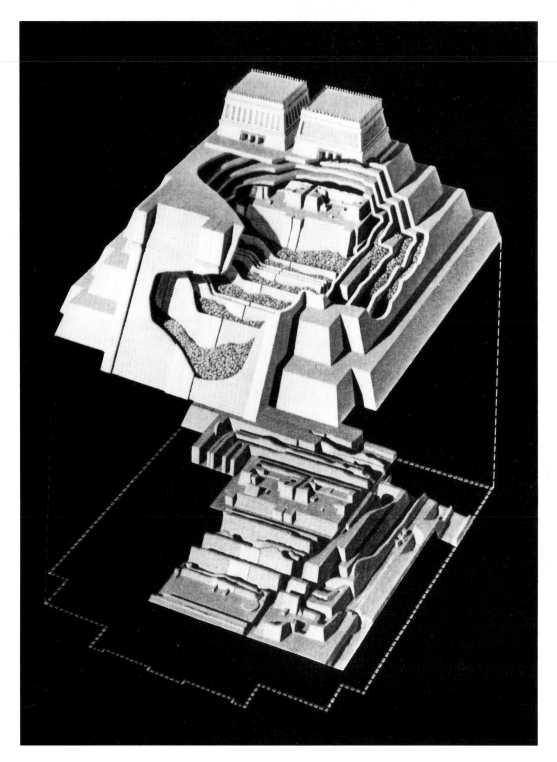

28 *The Great Temple of Tenochtitlan. Below, standing remains discovered in the excavations; above, reconstruction showing how earlier stages of the Temple were replaced by later ones superimposed directly on top.*

CHAPTER THREE

THE ARCHAEOLOGY OF THE GREAT TEMPLE

The discovery of the Coyolxauhqui relief in 1978 was a major event in the *14* history of Mexican archaeology. The realization that here was a keystone to the city's history caused the authorities to order intensive work to expose the central area of Tenochtitlan.

The Coyolxauhqui sculpture seemed to form part of the Great Temple (or *Huey Teocalli* in Nahuatl) itself. It was clear that all the explorations of the Temple undertaken during the first half of the twentieth century had examined only a very small part of the whole complex. To put the Coyolxauhqui Stone in its context, therefore, a research strategy involving thorough investigation of the urban environment surrounding the Temple was considered necessary. This would help to establish the aims of the project, the questions to be answered, and which archaeological techniques should be used. Three phases of research were proposed and eventually adopted.

Phase one: stating the problem

This consisted of gathering all information on the Great Temple currently available from both archaeological and historical sources. The limited archaeological investigation carried out on the Temple up until 1978 has already been outlined in the first chapter. In contrast, much more information about the structure was available from the eyewitness sixteenth-century accounts of chroniclers such as Bernal Díaz del Castillo and Hernán Cortés. According to the chronicles, the Great Temple was a pyramidal edifice facing west, with two stairways leading to its upper part. *28, 29* At the summit were two shrines, one dedicated to Tlaloc – god of rain, water, and the earth's fertility – and the other to Huitzilopochtli – solar

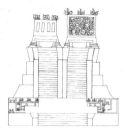

29 The Great Temple, crowned by the two shrines dedicated to Tlaloc and Huitzilopochtli. Codex Ixtlilxochitl.

and war god. These two gods were enshrined at that important spot because together they represented the Aztecs' most fundamental economic concerns: agriculture and tribute. The need for water was a major preoccupation which was the concern of Tlaloc, while warfare and military conquests, crucial for the maintenance and expansion of the Aztec empire, were overseen by Huitzilopochtli.

If it is accepted that agriculture and tribute were the pillars of Aztec economy and life, then it would seem reasonable to suggest that these things may be reflected in the architecture, sculptures, and offerings associated with the Great Temple. The team of archaeologists and specialists involved in the project, working within the restrictions of the urban setting, had to evaluate which excavation methods would be best for verifying or disproving this idea.

Phase two: the excavation

The excavation took place over five years, from 1978 to 1982. The modern urban environment not only presented the problem of how to deal with obstructions such as houses, streets, and drainage systems, but also meant that all the buildings in the proposed excavation area had to be assessed to avoid damaging those of historical significance. The downtown sector of the Great Temple is rich in colonial structures superimposed on Aztec remains. An Advisory Board on Monuments was established to decide which of the houses threatened by the excavation should be saved. As a result, only two of the buildings which were demolished had some sections dating to the colonial period, and these parts were photographed, numbered, and sent to the office in charge of Colonial Monuments.

30, 31, 35

Another important consideration was that the prehispanic buildings in the Great Temple area were severely damaged during the Spanish conquest and the stone re-used in colonial structures. For example, the latest construction stage of the Great Temple – there were found to be seven in all – had been leveled down to its foundations, and only traces of this stage were discovered on the flagstone floor of the great plaza of the ceremonial precinct, although at the north side of the square approximately 1 meter of the platform was well preserved. Construction from the earlier six stages, however, was found to be in much better condition, because these older, smaller levels were basically protected by later additions to the Great Temple, and were not intentionally razed; in fact the second construction stage (Stage II, AD 1390) was found almost complete.

General views of the excavations

30 (above) *View from the southwest showing the complicated layout of the multi-phase remains of the Great Temple. Note the Coyolxauhqui Stone under scaffolding near the center of the picture (see ill. 14).*

31 (right) *View from the south of the superimposed stairways of the Stage III (center) and Stage IV (left) Temple. The so-called "standard-bearers" are just visible at the foot of the Stage III steps (see ills. 112, 113 and color plate IX).*

The high modern water-table presented a further problem. It stands a mere 4–5 meters below present-day street level owing to the city's location over a lakebed. This meant that only the upper parts of the earlier levels of the Great Temple could be excavated, that is, the topmost of the four or five sloping tiers of the pyramidal core, and the remains of two shrines which surmounted it. If we had pumped out the water to reach the lower tiers it might have caused serious problems of stability not only for the Temple but also for the colonial and modern buildings near the precinct. Technological developments in future years may enable this subsurface water to be controlled and permit examination of the earlier levels. For the present, however, work was concentrated on the remains found above the water-table and below the streets of modern Mexico City.

To obtain the maximum information from the site a multidisciplinary approach was adopted. Biologists, chemists, and geologists from the Department of Prehistory of INAH were called in to help the archaeologists. Engineers specializing in soil mechanics were also consulted because of the problems of subsoil water, and they provided useful advice too on how close excavation trenches could be dug to nearby buildings without endangering them.

Anticipation of conservation needs was another important aspect of planning the excavation. Groups of technicians worked with the archaeologists, including photographers, draftsmen, and administrative assistants to record all the finds. Many of the objects and other remains required conservation, so a laboratory was set up with conservators working alongside archaeologists as they excavated architecture, murals, and offerings; in this way, a large amount of both organic and inorganic material was preserved.

The excavation covered a surface area of between 5,000 and 7,000 square meters and was divided into 2 × 2 meter grid squares, each square identified by a letter and number. Depth was gauged by carefully controlled measurements and a fixed starting point or datum. Excavation led to the third and final phase of analysis, that of interpretation of the results.

Phase three: results and interpretation

It appeared that the Great Temple had been constructed in seven stages, several of which could tentatively be dated by the glyphs carved on excavated objects. A brief explanation of this dating method seems appropriate here.

40–42

In Mesoamerica, two calendar systems were in use. The first of these was the 365-day cycle, the solar year, made up of 18 months of 20 days each (18 × 20 = 360) plus 5 additional days called *nemontemi*, which were considered to be a time of bad luck so that people stayed at home. Each month had a name and was celebrated with rites, and each day was both numbered and named. The second calendar system was the *Tonalpohualli* or 260-day cycle, a divinatory calendar composed of 20 day signs (for example, *Atl* = Water, *Acatl* = Reed, *Ollin* = Movement) which ran consecutively, combined with 13 numbers (20 × 13 = 260). When the 13 numbers were used up, number 1 started again but with a different sign, that is, with the fourteenth sign. Thus, if a day was designated as 5 *Calli* "5 House," in order for that same day 5 *Calli* to come around again, 260 days must elapse.

32

The two calendar rounds ran concurrently like interlocking wheels. When they met again at the starting point, 52 years had gone by, equivalent to our century. At that time the New Fire Ceremony was held so the next "century" could begin. The last New Fire Ceremony was celebrated in 1507 under Motecuhzoma II. The Aztec calendar has been synchronized with the Christian calendar on the basis of the date of Cortés' capture of Tenochtitlan – 13 August 1521, which was the year "3 House" and the day "1 Snake."[1]

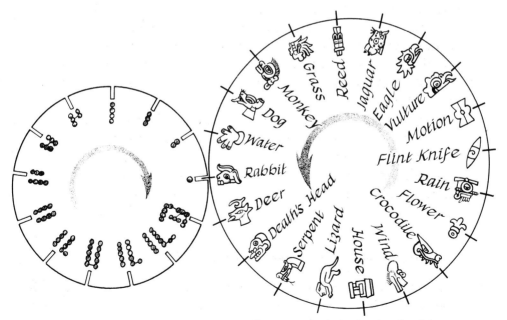

32 *Schematic representation of the "Tonalpohualli" or 260-day calendrical cycle of the Aztecs. The 20 day signs intermesh with the numbers 1 to 13.*

A year was named after the first day in it. Since the number of days in the solar year is 360 (+5), the 20 day names revolve constantly, always leaving the 5 *nemontemi* days at the end of the year. By dividing these 5 days into the 20 day names, only 4 will constantly turn up to begin a new year or any month. These 4 were called the "Year Bearers" and were *Acatl*, "Reed," *Tecpatl*, "Flint knife," *Calli*, "House," and *Tochtli*, "Rabbit."

The following discussion will focus on the architectural features and large sculptural finds from each of the seven construction stages; however, some of the sculptures that are specifically considered to be of Aztec manufacture will be detailed in the next chapter, together with the "offerings" from the Great Temple.

Construction Stage I

This can be identified with the sanctuary built by the Aztecs when they reached Tenochtitlan in AD 1325. This stage is known only from historical sources, because it was not possible to excavate below the Stage II pyramid owing to the high subsoil water-level.

Construction Stage II

Considerable information has come from the archaeological examination of Construction Stage II, and this is corroborated by historical accounts of the last or Stage VII Temple which the Spaniards saw and described. Numerous chronicles state that the Temple was crowned by two shrines dedicated to the gods Tlaloc and Huitzilopochtli. Bernal Díaz del Castillo describes the Great Temple thus:

33 *The two shrines at the summit of the Great Temple. In the one dedicated to Huitzilopochtli, on the right, the heart is being removed from a sacrificial victim whose blood cascades down the steps.*

In the shrines there were two figures, as if they were of giants, with very tall bodies, and very corpulent; and about the first, which was on the right side, they said it was Huichilobos [i.e. Huitzilopochtli], their god of war. . . At the summit of the Temple there was another recess made of richly carved wood, and here was another figure that seemed to be half man and half alligator . . . this body was covered with all the seeds of the earth, and they said this was the god of the fields and of the caves. . . [Tlaloc].[2]

Sahagún also describes the Temple:

This Temple was divided at the top so that it appeared to be two, and it had two shrines or altars at the summit, each one with its spire. And at the top each of these had its insignia or special emblems. In one of these shrines, the principal one, was the statue of Huitzilopochtli. . . . In the other, there was an image of the god Tlaloc. Before each one of these [images] there was a round stone like a chopping block, called *techcatl*, upon which they killed those who were sacrificed in honor of that god. And from these [sacrificial] stones to the base of the Temple flowed a stream of blood from those [victims] who were slain on them. And it was the same in all the other temples. These towers [i.e. temples] faced the west. The stairways were narrow and straight, from the base to the summit, on all these temples, all alike, and one ascended [the stairways, to reach the top].[3]

At the Temple's summit and in front of the entrance to Huitzilopochtli's shrine, a stone comparable to the one mentioned by the chroniclers was found *in situ* during the excavation of the Stage II structure, although this sacrificial stone was made of black *tezontle*, a volcanic rock. It was set into the floor 2 meters from the stairway and measured 50 × 45 centimeters, which is very close to the dimensions given by Sahagún when he refers to the stone used during a sacrifice in honor of Xipe Totec at the annual festival of Tlacaxipehualiztli: "When they reached the sacrificial block, which was a stone three *palmos* [about 24 inches or 60 centimeters high. . . and two *palmos* wide . . . they threw [the victims] over them, on their backs . . ."[4]

36, VIII

60

This stone would have served as a visual and functional symbol of Aztec power where war captives were slain. Sahagún would, of course, have seen a later stone to the one which was excavated here, and it may have been slightly larger, as well as of a different color, as Durán indicates:

Before the two rooms where these gods were found there was a courtyard 40 feet square, very well finished and painted white. In the middle [of this courtyard] and in front of those two rooms there was a green stone, rather pointed [in form], about as high as one's waist. And when a man was thrown on his back on this stone, his body bent over the stone; and thus they sacrificed men.[5]

This semi-precious stone used during the Temple's latest period was brought as tribute payment from areas in the present-day state of Guerrero, where it is very common.

At the entrance to the Tlaloc shrine of the Stage II Temple, and mirroring the location of the sacrificial stone in front of the Huitzilopochtli altar, a second sculpture, the multicolor *chacmool*, was discovered. This is a representation of a man, in a supine position, with a receptacle resting on his abdomen; his knees are bent and his head raised toward those approaching the shrine. The fact that the *chacmool* has been placed at the entrance in this way may corroborate one interpretation of the figure, namely that he represents a divine messenger, an intermediary bearing sacrifices and offerings between the priest and the gods.

It may be that both the sacrificial stone and the *chacmool* served as symbolic guardians for the Temple, and they may also reflect the character of the deity honored within each shrine. The sacrificial stone is more overtly associated with warfare and the fate of war captives, while the supine human figure is a more abstract, religious symbol signifying the divine intermediary.

Both shrines were originally decorated inside and out. Two stone pillars were found at the entrance to the Tlaloc shrine, and the outside faces of these bear geometric mural painting that symbolizes the deity: a band of "goggle-eyes" of Tlaloc painted black on a white background. Below these "eyes" is a horizontal strip of blue, followed by two red bands. The lower part of the pillars are painted with black and white vertical bands which may represent rain.

The remains of a wall were found at both ends of the shrine dedicated to Tlaloc, and it appears that it was originally divided into two long rooms. A banquette or low dividing wall lay in the center of the room, and perhaps the image of Tlaloc was placed on top of this bench.

Some of the interior painting from Tlaloc's shrine has survived. Standing human figures adorn the inner face of each of the two pillars; their bodies are painted yellow and they wear blue and black bracelets and leg ornaments. With legs apart as if striding, each figure extends his left arm with a staff or spear in his hand.

Huitzilopochtli's shrine was probably similar to the one dedicated to Tlaloc, at least in plan. Decoration on the bases of the two pillars has survived, as has some of the interior painting. A banquette was also found in the middle of this sanctuary, partly overlapped by a small altar – aligned with the sacrificial stone – on which the image of Huitzilopochtli once stood. This is corroborated by Durán, who remarks that this idol, thus

34 (opposite) Plan of the excavated remains of the Great Temple, showing how parts of five construction stages (II–VI) still survive.

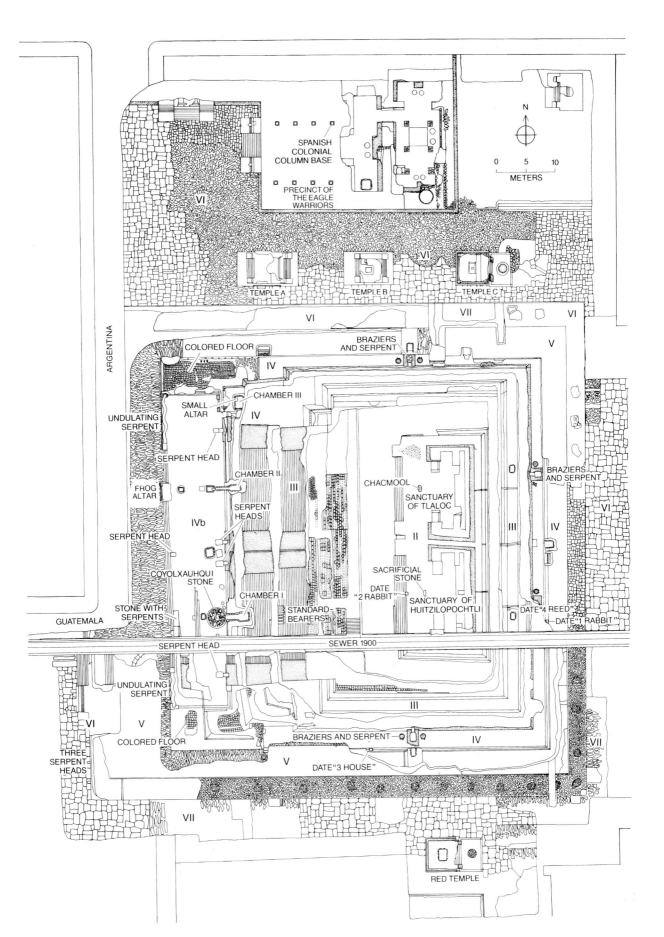

SPANISH
COLONIAL
COLUMN BASE

PRECINCT OF
THE EAGLE
WARRIORS

N

0   5   10
METERS

VI

VI

VI

TEMPLE A

TEMPLE B

TEMPLE C

ARGENTINA

VI

VII

VI

COLORED FLOOR

BRAZIERS
AND SERPENT

V

IV

CHAMBER III

SMALL
ALTAR

IV

UNDULATING
SERPENT

SERPENT HEAD

CHAMBER II

III

CHACMOOL

BRAZIERS
AND SERPENT

SANCTUARY
OF TLALOC

FROG
ALTAR

IVb

SERPENT
HEADS

III

IV

VI

SERPENT HEAD

II

COYOLXAUHQUI
STONE

CHAMBER I

SACRIFICIAL
STONE

STONE WITH
SERPENTS

STANDARD-
BEARERS

DATE
"2 RABBIT"

SANCTUARY OF
HUITZILOPOCHTLI

DATE "4 REED"

GUATEMALA

DATE "1 RABBIT"

SERPENT HEAD

SEWER 1900

UNDULATING
SERPENT

III

VI

V

IV

COLORED FLOOR

BRAZIERS AND SERPENT

THREE
SERPENT-
HEADS

V

DATE "3 HOUSE"

VII

VII

RED TEMPLE

The shrines of Tlaloc and Huitzilopochtli: the Stage II Temple

35 (above) Polychrome "chacmool" at the entrance to Tlaloc's shrine, holding a receptacle for the hearts of sacrificial victims.

36 (opposite, above) Detail of the top of the stairway on Huitzilopochtli's side of the Temple. Note the sacrificial stone in the background.

37 (opposite centre) Drawing of the summit of the Stage II Temple as excavated, showing the chacmool figure (ill. 35) in front of the shrine dedicated to Tlaloc (left-hand side), and the sacrificial stone at the entrance to Huitzilopochtli's shrine (right-hand side).

38 (opposite below) Wooden pillars being recovered from the entrance to Tlaloc's shrine.

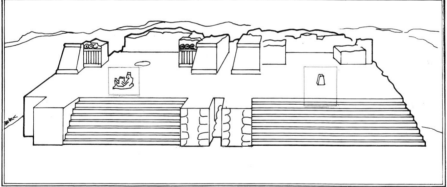

38   dressed and adorned, was always placed on a tall altar in a small room.[6]

Pine and cedar wood used for the door-jambs and pillars – and probably initially decorated – was found at the entrance to both shrines, as well as in a few of the offerings. Bernal Díaz del Castillo and Cortés (in his second *Carta de Relación*) both described richly decorated wood in the Temple interiors.

There are many reasons to believe that Stage II corresponds to the reigns of either Acamapichtli, Huitzilihuitl, or Chimalpopoca, that is, before 1428 (the year of Aztec independence from Azcapotzalco). The size of the Stage II Temple is markedly smaller than later constructions, suggesting an early date. Furthermore, on the top step of the stairway leading to the Huitzilopochtli shrine, and aligned with the sacrificial stone, a sculpted face with two glyphs above it was found. One glyph is almost completely destroyed, but the other represents the date "2 Rabbit," perhaps corresponding to AD 1390. Later construction stages were aimed at enlarging the Temple and so were built directly on top of this early edifice. However, only five of these construction stages were total enlargements on all four sides; others were enlargements of the main façade. The Temple described as Construction Stage II is the oldest structure found to date that has four sides.

36, VIII

Clearly a great quantity of fill was needed to cover this Stage II Temple in order to form a base for the following structures, in comparison with the fill required for subsequent building stages. This great surge of building activity gives the impression that, once liberated from the yoke of Azcapotzalco, the Aztecs wanted to construct a magnificent Temple – perhaps as a symbol of freedom.

It is known from historical sources that groups which paid tribute to the Aztecs brought *tezontle* and earth for constructional fill. The fact that the sacrificial stone was made of the same material used in construction attests to its early date because, as we have seen, greenstone – imported from southern Mexico – was used for the sacrificial block in the latest building stage.

Construction Stage III

Relatively little can be said about the construction of this stage because only the plain pyramidal base, without any adornment or surmounting

VIII *Detail of one of the steps at the top of the stairway leading to the shrine of Huitzilopochtli, Stage II. Above the sculpted face are two glyphs: one is indecipherable; the other reads "2 Rabbit," corresponding to* AD *1390.*

VIII

structures, has survived. The double stairways are well made and the walls forming the tiers of the pyramidal base are vertical. Eight *tezontle* sculptures, representing life-size standard-bearers, were found leaning against the steps near the base of the stairs leading to the Huitzilopochtli shrine. At one time they may have adorned the Temple; perhaps they represent Huitzilopochtli's brothers, the Huitznahua, and, when the new Temple was constructed, they were removed and placed ceremonially in a row on the stairway, to be covered up by the next construction stage.

On the back wall of the pyramidal body of the Great Temple, at the base of the side devoted to Huitzilopochtli, there is a stone carved with the calendrical glyph "4 Reed." This is probably equivalent to AD 1431, which would date this construction stage to the reign of Itzcoatl.

39 *The bows found on the braziers on Huitzilopochtli's side of the Temple are thought to represent this deity.*

Construction Stage IV

The architecture and sculptures of this stage are among the most spectacular known from the Great Temple. Not only is the pyramidal base enlarged, it is also adorned with braziers and serpent heads on all four sides. At the rear of the Tlaloc half of the Temple these over-sized braziers bear his face, while each of those on the Huitzilopochtli side – that is, the south façade – prominently display a large bow which is believed to be a symbol of this deity. Traces of various offerings are still evident, buried at the feet of these braziers and serpents, and will be described in the next chapter.

39, 54

75–77

Construction Stage IVb is labeled as such because it consists only of a partial enlargement of the Temple: the main façade, on the west side, was amplified and adorned with a wealth of different elements. The Temple from this stage rested on a vast platform with a single, majestic stairway. Enormous, undulating serpent bodies wrapped around the corners and terminated in dramatic snake heads, each one different from the next and several still showing traces of red, blue, and yellow pigment. The rise of the great stairway is broken only by a little altar near the base of the side dedicated to Tlaloc: two frogs rest on this altar, which has its own small steps and is aligned with the stairs leading to the shrine. In the middle of the stairway from the platform on the side of Huitzilopochtli's shrine there is a 2-meter-long tablet that forms part of the fourth step: it is made of andesite and has a serpent engraved on the rise.

108

43

IX *The standard-bearer sculptures found reclining against the stairway of the Stage III Temple leading to Huitzilopochtli's shrine. Average ht of figures 1.7 m. See also ills. 112, 113.*

44, 45   At the base of the platform formed by the remains of two stairways that originally rose to the top of the Temple, four serpent heads – two on the balustrades at either end and two in the middle – mark the place where the two structures dedicated to Tlaloc and Huitzilopochtli meet. In the middle 30 of Huitzilopochtli's side, at the foot of the stairway, Coyolxauhqui's dismembered body is preserved in low-relief carved on a huge stone.

34   The numerous offerings buried beneath this platform were either found around the Coyolxauhqui Stone, or between the two central serpent heads, or else at the base of the stairway on Tlaloc's side. Only Chambers X (caches) I and II were found behind this staircase, at the midway point of the sides dedicated to Huitzilopochtli and Tlaloc, respectively. Rooms paved with colored marble were discovered at the north and south ends of the Stage IVb platform, and on the north side of the platform two offerings appeared within a small altar with its own little stairway: one of these 47 offerings contained more than forty skulls and bones of children. Beneath 48, 49, XI this is the offering known as Chamber III; owing to their location and content, both these offerings appear to be dedicated to Tlaloc.

41   A stone plaque bearing the glyph "1 Rabbit" was found set in the back wall of the platform on Huitzilopochtli's side, and is believed to be equivalent to AD 1454.[7] Chronologically, therefore, it seems that Construction Stage IV corresponds to the reign of Motecuhzoma I. The Coyolxauhqui stone and the serpents may well have been added during Axayacatl's reign, judging from another relief on the south side of the 42 pyramid which bears the glyph "3 House:" this seems to relate to AD 1469, the year Axayacatl became *tlatoani*.

Glyphs dating the construction stages

40 (left) *Stage III glyph "4 Reed," corresponding to the year AD 1431, located at the rear of the Temple on Huitzilopochtli's side.*

41 (center) *Stage IV glyph "1 Rabbit," AD 1454, found on the back façade of the Temple, on Huitzilopochtli's side.*

42 (right) *Stage IVb glyph "3 House," AD 1469. This glyph is on the south wall of the Temple platform.*

Frogs and serpent heads on the Stage IVb Temple

43 (above) Frog altar, with serpent heads (ills. 44, 45) in the background, forming part of the pyramidal platform on the Tlaloc side of the Temple. The frog is a water and fertility symbol, closely linked with the rain god Tlaloc.

44, 45 Two views of the Great Temple platform where serpent heads mark the junction of the shrines of Tlaloc and Huitzilopochtli.

Offerings to Tlaloc, the rain god

46 (opposite) *Tlaloc vessel from offering 56, found on the north side of the Stage IV Temple. Ht 34 cm.*

47 (above) *Offering 48, found above Chamber III, with the skeletal remains of forty-two children sacrificed in honor of the water god. From the Stage IVb Temple.*

48 (right) *Chamber III with offerings in situ.*

49 (below) *Polychrome jar from Chamber III, dedicated to Tlaloc.*

Construction Stage V

Very little has survived from this stage. All that has been uncovered is the stucco plaster on the platform, and part of the floor of the ceremonial precinct, the latter formed by stone slabs joined by stucco.

Construction Stage VI

Part of the remains from what we can see of this penultimate building stage belong to the great platform underlying the whole of the Temple structure. As in all the previous periods, the main façade faces west. Part of the stairway is visible, but most of it was destroyed in 1900 when a large drainage ditch was cut through the Great Temple. Three serpent heads and a decorated balustrade adorn the principal façade.

51–53   The small temples on the north side of the Great Temple, the precinct of the Eagle warriors, and the large flagstone courtyard where these buildings are found, all belong to this construction stage. A temple similar to those on the north is found on the south side, and has been named "The Red Temple."

Each one of the temples to the north has distinctive features. These temples are designated by the letters A, B, and C, and will be briefly described:

Temple A. This shrine consists of a small pyramid which has two stairways, one oriented west, and the other east. The walls are covered with stucco but bear no decoration.

Temple B. This consists of a platform with straight walls and a single stairway facing east. The other three sides are decorated with rows of stone skulls: there are about 240 of these effigies, which were originally covered with various coats of stucco. The structure has been called a

55–57   *tzompantli*, or skull-rack altar; heads of those decapitated during certain
59, II   ceremonies would have been placed upon it.

50   Temple C. This shrine consists of a small rectangular structure enclosing a round altar, the front facing east. The side walls are decorated with *chalchihuitl*, modeled and painted red rings which represent water,

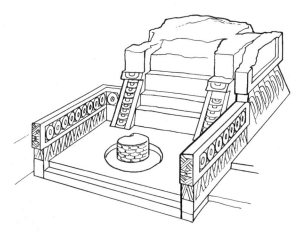

50 Temple C on the north side of the Great Temple.

The precinct of the Eagle warriors

51 (top) *The patio north of the Stage VI Great Temple pyramid revealed superimposed flagstones and the stairway leading to the precinct of the Eagle warriors.*

53 (above) *Detail of the stairway leading to the precinct.*

54 (left) *Brazier bearing the face of a "weeping" Tlaloc, found in the interior of the Eagle warriors' precinct.*

52 (above) *Interior of the precinct, showing the hall linking the entrance chamber to a series of rooms in the rear.*

Temple B, the skull-rack altar

55 (opposite) *The skull-rack altar, or "tzompantli," located at the north of the Stage VI Great Temple complex. It may represent the north quadrant of the four world quarters, the direction associated with the Land of the Dead.*

56, 57 (above) *Views of the sculpted skull-rack façade.*

58 (left) *Offering H, found within the altar. This offering is typical of those placed in cists. Among the objects interred were musical instruments, a Tlaloc effigy vessel, and jaguar remains.*

81

Templo del ydolo Vitzilo puestli.

59 *The Great Temple and the skull-rack, or "tzompantli." Codex Durán.*

symbolizing something precious. A stairway rises at the back of the enclosure. The building is completely covered with decoration, principally in red and white pigment. Both the *talud* and *tablero* profile (sloping walls and vertical panels) of the shrine, and the wall decoration, are reminiscent of the architecture and mural painting of Teotihuacan, the great metropolis that dominated Central Mexico from the second to eighth centuries AD. These possible associations with Teotihuacan will be discussed in more detail in the next chapter.

Forming part of this complex of three temples in the northern section, a large pyramidal platform faces west and is known as the precinct of the Eagle warriors, where outstanding soldiers of the nobility would have gathered. The name is derived from representations of the head of an eagle – still showing signs of paint – on each of its balustrades. The western

52, 53

façade joins up with another one looking south, in a courtyard we have called "The Eagle Patio." The floor on which these structures stand is *51* made up of various superpositions and is still in magnificent condition.

According to Sahagún, there were seventy-eight structures, including the Great Temple, within the sacred space of the ceremonial precinct,[8] which measured 500 meters on each of its four sides. The patio at the rear of the Temple, which would have formed part of this sacred space, is made of flat stones joined by stucco, and dates to Construction Stage VI. Sections of stairway alternating with fragments of balustrade form the eastern limit of the ceremonial precinct, a boundary device similar to that found at Tlatelolco: this archaeological discovery, however, contradicts some of the chroniclers who claimed that a wall in the form of serpents encircled the precinct.

Construction Stage VII
This is the final building stage of the Great Temple and is the one seen by the Spaniards at the beginning of the sixteenth century. All that remains of this period is part of the stone flooring of the ceremonial precinct and traces of where the Temple stood. Part of the platform belonging to Stage VI is still visible on the north side; but the three shrines (A, B, and C) and the Eagle precinct were completely covered by the flooring of this final building stage.

The multidisciplinary approach discussed at the beginning of this chapter is also being employed in the interpretation of the archaeological finds. Biologists are analyzing faunal remains while other specialists are studying, for example, the North Patio, the Mezcala-style stone masks and figurines, and the rich contents of one particular offering, designated number 48. The next chapter examines the offerings from the Great Temple in more detail.

CHAPTER FOUR

TREASURES FROM
THE GREAT TEMPLE

More than one hundred offerings were found during the Great Temple excavations. Some of these were discovered outside the Temple itself, in nearby shrines, but it is the characteristics of the offerings associated directly with the main Temple that will be discussed here.

These offerings were found in three contexts: in cists – small chambers with stone walls and floors covered with stucco remains; inside stone boxes with stone covers; or placed directly in the nucleus of the earth and rubble fill which covered an earlier construction. The majority of the offerings were concentrated beneath the front platform of the Great Temple and in the immediate areas of the twin shrines. In general, they appeared to be oriented along certain axes. For example, in an east–west direction, three principal axes are formed, two by lines running one each through the Tlaloc and Huitzilopochtli shrines and their respective stairways, and one through the middle of the Great Temple where the two halves join. In a north–south direction, the main axis crosses approximately at the middle of the building at the level of the serpent heads and braziers on the north and south façades. Offerings were also placed equidistantly around the pyramidal platform, as well as in its four corners.

Funerary urns found were classed as offerings in the project's nomenclature, but were actually more related to mortuary ritual (offerings 10, 14, 30, and 34).

There appear to be patterns in the orientation of certain offerings. Those on both the west and east sides of the Temple – the front and back respectively – are oriented toward the west, the setting sun, whilst offerings found at the middle of the building, on the north and south façades, are oriented north and south respectively.

60 Stone head of Xipe Totec, the flayed god associated with vegetation, wearing his flayed skin. Ht 11.9 cm.

58

34

93, XIV

Offering 7 from the Stage IV Temple

61–63 Plans of levels I, II, and III.

64 (below left) Vertical section of offering 7, showing its relationship to one of the serpent heads on the Temple platform.

PLATFORM

0 10 20 30 50   100 cms

CIST-OFFERING 7

65 *Level I of offering 7 (cf. ill. 61), the contents of which are similar to those of offering 61 (ills. 66, 67). Note the figure of the Old God of Fire in the center.*

Placement of objects within the offerings was clearly premeditated, although the symbolic meaning behind the artifacts, including their arrangement, remains undeciphered. Offering 7, located in the middle of the Temple on the south façade, and offering 61 – on the north side – display identical distributions of artifacts. (In addition, two other offerings, both placed in stone-walled cists, also have a similar arrangement of their contents: these are offering 11, located on the main façade between the two serpent heads which mark the juncture between the shrines dedicated to Tlaloc and Huitzilopochtli; and offering 17, found at the rear of the Temple, where these two shrines meet.) In both offerings 7 and 61 the lowest level was composed of strombus shells, oriented north to south; this was overlain by crocodile remains, and on top of these were figures of the seated god whose interpretation is much disputed, but whom I have called Xiuhtecuhtli, the fire-deity represented as an old man (see below). Coral was placed on the right side of these sculptures, and on their left was positioned a clay vessel with an effigy of the god Tlaloc.

This hierarchy of space may be related to the hierarchy of the objects themselves, or to their owners. Perhaps the shells represent the sea, the

61–65
66, 67

81

66, 67 Offering 61, on the Tlaloc side of the Stage IV Temple, showing topmost (left) and bottommost (right) levels. Among the contents were vessels with Tlaloc effigies, a crocodile skull, a representation of the Old God of Fire, and coral.

crocodiles a terrestrial level, and Xiuhtecuhtli and Tlaloc the celestial level? Chapter 5 will address this question. Analysis of these offerings may help not only to corroborate the chronology of the Great Temple but also to clarify the symbolic and contextual meaning behind the artifacts, thus giving us a wider understanding of Aztec beliefs.

Let us now turn to a more detailed examination of the contents of the eighty-six offertory caches found directly associated with the Great Temple. More than 6,000 objects were excavated from these offerings; some pieces were clearly of Aztec manufacture but most came from tribute-paying regions. The Aztec empire extended from the modern states of Veracruz, Hidalgo, Morelos, and Guerrero, down to Oaxaca, with

X Offerings discovered in Chamber II in the Stage IV Temple. Note the greenstone figure of Tlaloc in the center (see ill. 74).

XI

XII

68 *Map showing the extent of the Aztec empire,* AD *1519.*

isolated pockets of independent polities in Michoacan, Tlaxcala, and   68
parts of Puebla. The majority of "foreign" – non-Aztec – articles in the
offerings came from areas under the control of Tenochtitlan, whereas not
a single artifact from the Tarascan culture of Michoacan appeared,
because this was a territory the Aztecs were unable to conquer. Similarly,
no materials from the Maya region were unearthed.[1]

The greatest number of offerings was found between Construction
Stages IV and V, corresponding roughly to the period from AD 1440, when
Motecuhzoma I took the throne until after AD 1469, the beginning of
Axayacatl's reign (Stage IVb). This brief time-span was one of great
military expansion by the Aztecs, which is clearly reflected in the
exceptionally rich contents of the offerings from this stage, in contrast to
the deposits of earlier and later stages.[2] In fact some 80 per cent of the
objects found in these offerings are from tribute-paying areas, while
materials that may be classified as truly Aztec are scant.

The following discussion of the offerings discovered during the most
recent excavations will be divided into four sections: objects of Aztec
material; objects from tributary regions; artifacts belonging to cultures
prior to the Aztecs; and, finally, faunal remains – which are principally
from the Mexican gulf and Pacific regions, and only to a lesser extent from
the local central highland environment.

XI, XII *Polychrome jars, stone masks, and other offerings found in Chamber III beneath the
Stage IVb Temple. Ht of jar 40 cm.*

Aztec material

The quantity of Aztec artifacts found at the Great Temple is small compared with that of foreign objects. However, the quality of these pieces is striking and shows that, despite their humble beginnings, the Aztecs were not to be outdone by their neighbors. This is especially true of stone sculpture and smaller lapidary objects.

The most standardized and abundant artifacts are a series of volcanic stone sculptures of a deity of much disputed identity. These images depict 69–72 a seated man, wearing only a breechcloth and headdress, with two projections rising from his crown. Two blunt fang-like teeth protrude from his mouth and are indicative of his old age. The identity of this figure has long been the subject of scholarly discussion, and several interpretations have been proposed.

The god Tepeyolotl, "Heart of the Mountain," an aspect of the deity Tezcatlipoca, is represented in the Borgia (14) and Borbonicus (3) codices.[3] There are marked similarities in dress and accoutrements between this god and the images found at Tenochtitlan, and so Henry B. Nicholson suggests that the representations are one and the same.

The inclusion of this sculpture in burial offerings supposedly symbolizes the "heart" of the offering within the Great Temple, the supreme idol among the Aztecs. Also based on a study of the costume attributes, Debra Nagao identifies this sculpture as the supreme deity Tonacatecuhtli, "Lord of Sustenance," a creator god also known as Ometeotl, "Sacred Two," progenitor of the universe.[4] According to her interpretation, the Great Temple was symbolically identified as the source of sustenance for the Aztec empire and as Omeyocan, the supreme center of the universe and the highest of all realms.

Despite the persuasive evidence provided by these and other investigators, my view is that the sculpture represents the god Xiuhtecuhtli, the Old God of Fire. The two projections from the figure's head perhaps symbolize fire sticks, a crucial costume element that identifies Xiuhtecuhtli in the Borbonicus (9, 20). My viewpoint is not incompatible with those previously expressed, because it seems that the Xiuhtecuhtli sculpture was buried in the Great Temple offerings for very specific symbolic reasons linked to the concepts of heart and center.

The Old God of Fire (opposite)

69 (above left) *Offering 24, Stage IVb. Detail showing part of the remains of a sawfish together with a sculpture of the Old God of Fire, Xiuhtecuhtli. This type of offering was placed in the fill of a construction stage.*

70 (above right) *Another offering from Stage IVb, containing a stone sculpture of Xiuhtecuhtli, a Tlaloc vessel, and coral remains.*

71, 72 (below) *Rear and front views of a stone sculpture of the Old God of Fire. Ht 32 cm.*

Xiuhtecuhtli lived in the center of the universe, symbolized by the Great Temple, and was the father of the gods; he was said to reside in the "navel" of the world, the center and source for all life. The role of this important god needs further explanation.

Xiuhtecuhtli was the God of Fire but his name is translated both as "Turquoise Lord" (referring to the blue flame in fire, and also to the "turquoise enclosure" at the center of the earth where Xiuhtecuhtli was said to dwell), and as "Lord of the Year," since *xiuhuitl* means "year, turquoise, fire." He was the archetype of the rulers "who were preferably consecrated and confirmed in their public affairs on his special calendric sign, 4 *Acatl* (4 "Reed")," according to H. B. Nicholson.[5]

The characteristics of prehispanic Aztec deities were never clear cut, one god often overlapping another. In Xiuhtecuhtli's case, he merged both with Ometeotl (the creator pair) as *Teteo innan, Teteo inta,* "Mother and Father of the Gods," and with Tezcatlipoca, who was also a patron of rulers. His relationship with Huitzilopochtli can be seen in that the Aztec god-leader's magic weapon was the *xiuhcoatl,* "turquoise (fire) serpent," which was also an insignia of Xiuhtecuhtli. As a recent god in the Aztec pantheon, Huitzilopochtli, who must have been a human leader, later deified, seems to have absorbed traits of older gods, such as Xiuhtecuhtli and Tezcatlipoca. Possibly the closest association between Xiuhtecuhtli and Huitzilopochtli, however, may be that both were gods dedicated to rulers and lords.

While Xiuhtecuhtli, or Tepeyolotl-Tonacatecuhtli occupies the most honored position in Aztec offerings, the most frequently represented deity
46   at the Great Temple is Tlaloc, god of rain and the earth's fertility.
73, 74 Sometimes he is identified simply by representations of his face, with its characteristic "goggle-eyes," twisted serpent nose, and fanged mouth, or else he is shown as a full-figure effigy.

Aztec representations of Tlaloc are mainly stone jars bearing his head, made of *tezontle.* Eleven vessels of this type, averaging 30 centimeters in height, were found in the upper part of offering 48, located on the Tlaloc or north side of the Great Temple and corresponding to Stage IVb (*c.* AD 1469). These jars still show remains of blue paint, a color appropriate to the water deity. Beneath these Tlaloc vessels, the skeletal remains of at
47   least forty-two infants were discovered, undoubtedly sacrificed in honor of the god. Sahagún mentions infantile sacrifices to Tlaloc at certain festivals.[6]

Perhaps one of the most valuable representations of Tlaloc is a full-
74, X figure image carved from a solid block of greenstone, one of the Aztecs'

Tlaloc effigies

73 *Left to right: polychrome stone head from the Stage VI Temple, ht 53 cm; ceramic vessel, Stage IVb, ht 18 cm; stone vessel, Stage IV, offering 17, ht 21 cm.*

74 (left) *Greenstone figure of Tlaloc found in Chamber II in the Stage IVb Temple. Ht 31 cm.*

75–77 *Stone braziers, two* (above left *and* below left; *ht 11 cm*) *adorned with a bow, one of Huitzilopochtli's symbols, the third* (above; *ht 1 m*) *found built into the Tlaloc (north) side of the Great Temple and bearing the face of the rain god.*

most precious commodities. Approximately 31 centimeters high, this figure must have been valued for its religious as well as its economic significance. It was one of the main deity images interred in the rich cache in Chamber II, a deposit located beneath the front platform on the Tlaloc half of the Great Temple. The fine greenstone from which the figure is fashioned comes from southern Mexico, but the sculpting may have been done by an Aztec artist.

Images of various other deities have also been found among the offerings at the Great Temple. A large greenstone tablet, 1.4 meters long, was found in the Chamber I cache, on the Huitzilopochtli (southern) side of the Temple. The raw material of this spectacular piece was not locally available and was acquired from southern Mexico, but the craftsmanship appears to be completely Aztec. The surface was engraved with the image of a female figure. Alfredo Lopez Austin claims that the deity represented is Mayahuel, goddess both of the *maguey* cactus (century plant) and of *pulque*, an intoxicating ritual beverage made from this plant.[7] Two other vessels, from offerings 6 and 20, also made of greenstone and approximately 16 centimeters high, bear the image of yet another deity. A full-length skeletal figure is masterfully sculpted on each vessel to represent Mictlantecuhtli, "Lord of the Land of the Dead."

The presence of the patron god Huitzilopochtli in the offerings is perhaps indicated by the small stone braziers, adorned with a bow tied in front. These braziers vary in size: some, 20 centimeters high, are often made of volcanic stone, while others, made either in the same material or of basalt, can be smaller, averaging 15 centimeters. Brazier effigies are *75, 76* known from many offerings, and my view is that the knotted bow ornament does indeed refer to Huitzilopochtli. Large bows adorn the full- *39* sized braziers that stood on the Huitzilopochtli side of the Temple platform, as discussed in the last chapter, while Tlaloc faces were displayed on the braziers on the Temple's north side. This symbolism may *77* also be applied to the small-scale artifacts used as offerings.

Many objects of flint and obsidian, locally available raw materials, were also made by Aztec artisans to be deposited in caches. Flint was most frequently chipped into knives and blades. Some of these knives were decorated with bits of shell and stone mosaic to form little faces in profile, *XXI–XXIII* resembling representations of the flint day sign in the Borbonicus (4). Similarly, obsidian (a volcanic glass) was chipped to form knives and blades with sharp cutting edges, but it was also carefully worked and polished into miniature imitations, such as small heads and rattles of the *78* rattlesnake. Obsidian is an extremely dense and glassy stone, and is a difficult material to work; such miniatures attest to the skill of the Aztec craftsmen.

While flint and obsidian implements symbolically and functionally evoke sacrifice and death, more overt evidence of ritual acts can be found in the numerous examples of worked human crania. These take the form of the "skull mask," and consist of only the front half of the cranium, *79* including the jaw bone. The eye sockets are filled with white shell disks, with round pieces of hematite for the iris. Small holes are drilled around the perimeter of the forehead, perhaps for the attachment of other materials. Sometimes a flint knife is placed between the teeth, like a tongue *80, 81* projecting from a grinning mouth, at other times another knife is inserted into the nasal cavity to create an animated image of death. We do not know whether these objects were used as masks in rituals, or whether they were made as symbols of death and sacrifice to be placed in offerings.

78 Obsidian head and rattle of a rattlesnake, made by an Aztec artisan. From the Stage IVb Temple. L. 5 cm.

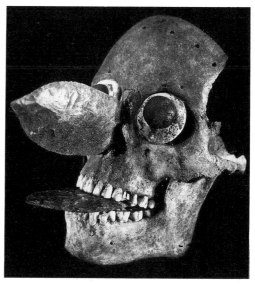

Skull masks

79, 80 Human skulls, from Stage IVb offerings, with eye sockets inlaid with shell and hematite and (right, from offering 11, see ill. 81) with flint knives in the nasal cavity and mouth.

81 Excavation of offering 11, which was placed directly in the fill covering one of the earlier construction stages.

82 *Stone sculpture of a conch shell found behind the Great Temple. Ht 74.5 cm.*

A very different kind of mask is a striking one made of alabaster, another highly regarded material. Although evidently an Aztec mask, it was found in offering 82, along with a Teotihuacan-style mask, which will be discussed later.

Among the exciting and important Aztec objects not found in offerings, there are numerous examples of stone sculpture. Perhaps the most sensational piece is the colossal stone Coyolxauhqui relief, 3.25 meters in diameter. This relief was undoubtedly one of the most important specimens of Aztec sculpture.

Three huge, superbly executed sculptures, representing conch shells, were found in the patio behind the Great Temple. They give the impression of great simplicity, but on closer examination every line is found to be true to life. Specimens from nature copied by Aztec artisans can often be identified by modern biologists.

Another impressive sculpture that came to light is a large representation of Huehueteotl, whose name means "Old God," an aspect of Xiutecuhtli. He sits in a hunched position and bears a large brazier on his head. Many block-shaped images of this deity are known from the city of Teotihuacan during the Classic period (AD 0–750), but none compare with this finely carved, elaborate version from the Aztec Great Temple. This statue was excavated in the northern part of the Great Temple complex, near Temple C, which itself bears a resemblance to Teotihuacan architecture. Both the

83 *Conch shell trumpets were used in ritual performances. Codex Magliabechiano.*

84, 85

84, 85 Stone sculpture of the "Old God," Huehueteotl. In the illustration above, Professor Matos is shown excavating the figure, which was found near Temple C.

sculpture and the small temple correspond to Construction Stage VI, approximately AD 1500. Perhaps the Aztec Huehueteotl sculpture originally stood on top of this small shrine. Aztec versions of Teotihuacan-style architecture and sculpture reflect the reverence in which they held that great city, home of their sacred ancestors and gods.

The most magnificent and perhaps surprising sculptural finds were two unique masterpieces of the potter's art, life-size images of men wearing eagle costumes which were found flanking the entrance to a series of rooms to the north of the Great Temple complex. Very few human-scale clay images are known from prehispanic Mesoamerica; this may be due to the technical difficulties presented by the manufacture of statues of this size. Each figure was made in four sections. The head with eagle helmet has a tenon which fits into a mortise in the second portion, consisting of the

VII

torso with bent and extended arms displaying eagle's wings. The next section, from the waist to the thighs, was also joined to the lower leg with mortise and tenon. Eagle claws were modeled on the calves of the figure, while remains of white clay on the upper leg area represented feathers. Based on the costume, these two figures probably portrayed Eagle warriors. The two leading military orders in Aztec society, the Jaguar knights and Eagle knights, have already been mentioned; they were made up of the bravest soldiers of noble birth and of those who had taken the greatest number of prisoners in battle. The "Eagles" were soldiers of the sun, for the eagle was the sun's symbol. These images stood guard over the precinct that was probably the *sanctum sanctorum* of the Eagle military order (see page 82). The structures, as well as the sculptures, date to Construction Stage V, about AD 1485, although the precinct was further built upon in Construction Stage VI.

Material from tribute-paying regions

While non-Aztec objects are much more abundant than locally produced items in offertory caches, they seem to fall into discrete groupings of common object types; in only a few instances are there foreign objects that may be considered unique. The vast majority of non-Aztec articles come 68 from southern Mexico (today's state of Guerrero), but many other previously mentioned regions are represented as well, including the modern states of Veracruz, Oaxaca, and Puebla. These artifacts were not all necessarily the result of tribute; it may be that some items were acquired through trade or ceremonial exchange between rulers.

We know that many southern Mexican towns were conquered during the reigns of Motecuhzoma I and Axayacatl. A large number of masks and figurines from this area, carved mainly of greenstone, came to light in the cache known as Chamber II on Tlaloc's side of the Great Temple, 86 Construction Stage IV; fifty-six human figurines were excavated. (In total, 87–92 some 162 masks and 220 figurines from southern Mexico were found during the project and it is interesting to note that almost all the offerings contained at least a few pieces from Guerrero.) Stylistic analysis of these objects, and of the types of greenstone used to make them, is currently in progress.[8] These masks and figurines are often described as "Mezcala-style," named after the region in Guerrero where most of the material was probably mined. A hallmark of the style is the angular, schematic

86 Stone masks and other offerings in Chamber II, discovered beneath the stairway on the Tlaloc side of the Stage IV Temple.

Stone masks

87 (above left) *Human figurine carved in stone.*

88 (above) *Human figure carved in greenstone, from the Guerrero area. Stage IVb. Ht 28 cm.*

89 (left) *Human figure carved in stone, from the state of Guerrero. Stage IVb, offering 6. Ht 28 cm.*

90 (opposite, above) *Stone mask representing Tlaloc, from the southern tributary areas. Stage IVb, offering 6. Ht 16.7 cm.*

91 (opposite, left) *Stone mask from the Guerrero area. Stage IVb, offering 41. Ht 28.5 cm.*

92 (opposite, right) *Guerrero-style stone mask with shell and obsidian inlays, from the southern tributary provinces. Stage IVb, offering 11. Ht 21.6 cm.*

treatment of shapes, which are transformed into extremely simplified and often geometric forms. There appear to be various distinct styles within this umbrella heading; perhaps a stylistic and petrographic study of this type could define more precisely other local styles in Guerrero.

93, XIV   Two magnificently incised ceramic funerary urns, containing cremations, are probably from the present-day state of Veracruz.[9] Although these masterpieces were found in separate offertory caches – approximately 1 meter apart – under the floor of Construction Stage IVb, near the huge Coyolxauhqui relief, they seem to form a pair. They share an identical form and raw material and show similarities in pose, costume, and attributes to the deities adorning the vessels. Both are made of orange clay burnished to a high finish, with a prominent pedestal base and plain lid, and are about 33 centimeters high and 17.5 centimeters in diameter. H. B. Nicholson and Eloise Keber[10] have made the interesting observation that this vessel type strongly resembles a common Fine Orange ceramic form, a ware widespread during Toltec times and from somewhere on the Gulf Coast, further strengthening Veracruz origins for these pieces.

The symbolic content of these vessels is complex and disputed. The body of each urn is engraved with the image of a standing, armed deity. Both gods wear a breechcloth, carry a spearthrower and spears, and behind each figure rears an undulating serpent. One of the gods is easily identified as Tezcatlipoca, for he bears a smoking mirror replacing one foot, the distinctive characteristic of this deity. The identity of the other deity is more uncertain. Based on costume and symbolic details, he has been identified as various different gods: Xiuhtecuhtli, because of the stepped pectoral ornament prominently displayed on his chest; Quetzalcoatl, due to the sliced conch shell motif along the border; and Mixcoatl, because of the two feathers set into a ball of down in his headgear. Perhaps he is a composite of all three divinities.

As well as charred bones, both vessels contained various other artifacts; those within the Tezcatlipoca urn comprised fourteen obsidian beads in the form of ducks' heads, two long stone beads, and two spear points. In the other urn, a greenstone serpentiform pectoral was found. Because these vessels were located near the relief of Coyolxauhqui, the female warrior of myth, and on the side of the Temple associated with Huitzilopochtli, the principal Aztec war god, I would argue that the cremations may have been those of outstanding Aztec military captains, honored by interment in the pyramidal base of the Great Temple.

XIII *Stone sculpture of the Old God of Fire, Xiuhtecuhtli. Ht 32 cm.*

Ceramic funerary urns from the Stage IVb Temple

93 Urn bearing the representation of the god Tezcatlipoca. Ht 32.9 cm.

XIV (opposite) *Urn with engraved representation of the god Mixcoatl-Quetzalcoatl.
Ht 33.2 cm.*

94, 95 Offering 34 from the Stage II Temple yielded this 9.8-cm-high obsidian funerary urn (far right), *containing a tiny gold bell* (near right), *a silver maskette* (color plate XVIII), *and other items.*

96 (opposite) *Stone figurines representing Tlaloc, the first two (12 cm high) sculpted by Mixtec artisans and discovered in the Stage IVb Temple.*

Two of the pieces from the earliest excavated level of the Great Temple, Construction Stage II, are also funerary urns. These were found beneath the floor of the shrine dedicated to Huitzilopochtli; one was deposited below the precise spot where the statue of the god must have stood. One of the vessels, 9.8 centimeters high and 4.8 centimeters in diameter, and its lid, is made entirely of carved and polished obsidian. Its only ornamentation consists of a skull-like face projecting from one side. Within this small urn were a little silver maskette with simian features and rattlesnake-shaped ear ornaments, a tiny gold bell with an *ollin* or "movement" symbol, cremated human bones, and copal resin, a type of incense used in ritual.

The other urn, 17 centimeters high and 9.5 centimeters in diameter, is made of alabaster, but is covered by an oddly shaped, polished lid. This vessel is carved to form a body, with awkward, jutting arms and legs, and

94

XVIII

95

blocky, projecting head, which appears to bear the "goggle eyes" of the deity Tlaloc. As well as cremated human bones, the vessel contained a gold bell and two flat greenstone beads. It is possible that the all-obsidian urn and lid are of Aztec manufacture; the existence of a tradition of carved and polished obsidian artifacts, represented by other Great Temple finds, was suggested in the preceding section. However, it is more difficult to determine the provenience of the alabaster vessel for it does not resemble other artifacts of known Aztec or even non-Aztec style.

Several cached objects are clearly from the modern-day state of Oaxaca. A number of stone sculptures, generally measuring between 10 and 20 centimeters, are from the Mixtec region in the northwestern part of Oaxaca. These small-scale images, some representing Tlaloc, are believed to have been "penates," or household gods. Much more spectacular Mixtec-style objects are the elaborate multicolored effigy vessels found in

96

97, 99 Life-size stone masks found in offering 82, part of the Stage IV Temple. (right) Teotihuacan-style inlaid greenstone mask, with earspools on either side. (opposite) Alabaster mask of Aztec manufacture.

98 Alabaster rattle staff or spear point, from offering 24, Stage IVb. L. 11.9 cm.

offertory cache Chamber III, located in the platform on the Tlaloc side of the Temple. These vessels bear the modeled visage of a corn deity, holding stalks of maize in both hands. On the brightly painted lid is a representation of Tlaloc.

A variety of small-scale lapidary artifacts are believed to come from beyond the Valley of Mexico, but still within the central highlands. Alabaster, fashioned into the form of miniature deer-headed staffs and tiny rattlestaffs (used in ceremonies to attract rain) which at first glance seem to be elaborate spear points or solar rays, was found in numerous offertory caches. Alabaster may have been mined in the present-day states of Mexico or Puebla; both areas came under Aztec control during the reigns of Motecuhzoma I and Axayacatl.[11] Several ceramic Tlaloc effigy vessels also perhaps come from the Puebla or southern Tlaxcala region. These vessels, approximately 35 centimeters high, are painted in a vibrant sky blue with some white and red details, and have elaborate appliqué faces. Doris Heyden, comparing the unique serpentine designs surrounding the eyes and mouth with the snake markings in the Codex

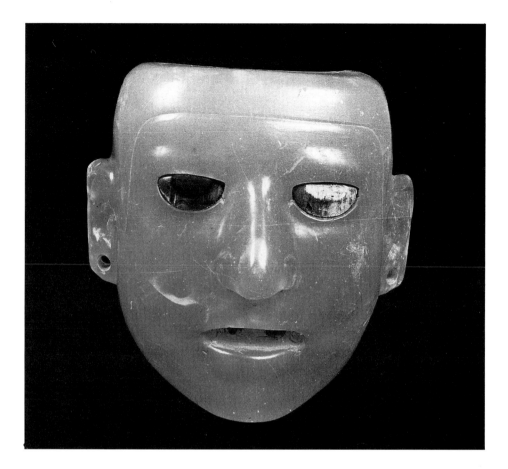

Borgia group, believes that both the vessels and the manuscripts have the same provenience, which is widely ascribed to the Puebla-Tlaxcala area.[12]

Objects from earlier cultures

In addition to Aztec imitations of earlier forms and styles, referred to in the previous sections on Aztec and foreign artifacts, a few specimens of true "antiques" were found in the offerings. These lapidary objects, exemplifying major pre-Aztec styles, demonstrate that the Aztecs were, to a certain extent, aware and perhaps in awe of great civilizations of the past. Such pieces were found in offertory caches together with Aztec and foreign items; it appears that the old was indiscriminately mixed with the new.

The oldest piece to have come out of the offerings is a small Olmec-style   XV greenstone maskette, 10.5 centimeters high and 8.6 centimeters wide, believed to date to around 800 BC – some two millennia prior to the rise of the Aztec empire. It bears typical Olmec features, such as the V-shaped cleft in the head and inverted U-shaped mouth. Petrographic analysis of the greenstone has indicated origins around the region of Puebla, Oaxaca, and Guerrero. Although the "heartland" of the Olmec civilization is traditionally placed in the area of Tabasco, it is clear that Olmec cultural and stylistic traits were dispersed far beyond the central core zone.[13]

97, 99   Several Teotihuacan-style lapidary masks have been found in different offerings, but one is outstanding for the quality of its workmanship. Excavated in offering 82, from the southeast corner of Construction Stage IV, this fine greenstone piece was associated with an Aztec alabaster mask. The Teotihuacan-style mask, 20 centimeters high and 21 centimeters wide, was found directly on top of a human cranium, with a large round earspool on each side of the head. The face of the mask is highly animated: the shell and obsidian inlays forming the eyes – and the red and white shell carefully worked into teeth – contrast with the dark greenstone of the mask. This pre-Aztec piece is believed to date to around AD 500, when the city of Teotihuacan was at its height. The recent excavations were not the first time that Teotihuacan material was discovered in Tenochtitlan; when Leopoldo Batres excavated in the Great Temple at the beginning of this century he also found material from the great Classic site, and more continues to appear in contemporary excavations.[14]

The discovery of these ancient objects raises various questions. Why were these pieces, antiques at the time of the Aztec empire, placed in offertory caches at the Great Temple? And how did they get to Tenochtitlan?

In the case of objects from Teotihuacan, there is ample evidence to suggest the importance of this site to the Aztecs. Just northeast of the Valley of Mexico, it was regarded as a sacred and powerful place. We do not know the original name of this city, for "Teotihuacan" is an Aztec designation, which in Nahuatl means "the place where gods (or rulers) are made." According to Aztec myths, the sun was born in Teotihuacan, and it was here that the gods sacrificed themselves so that the sun could absorb their life-blood and thus have the energy to cross the sky. The proximity of Teotihuacan to Tenochtitlan made it a very conveniently located holy spot, and Aztec rulers went there to worship every twenty days.[15] The grandeur of this huge ancient metropolis and its pyramidal mounds was no doubt an impressive and awesome spectacle to the Aztecs, so perhaps it is not surprising that many myths centering on Teotihuacan were created.

84, 85   Aztec architectural and sculptural references to Teotihuacan have already been mentioned and include the large Huehueteotl sculpture, and
50   the Red Temple and Temple C, located at the south and north sides of the

Great Temple respectively. These small shrines demonstrate the characteristic Teotihuacan *talud* and *tablero* profile, consisting of a sloping wall combined with a rectangular vertical panel. They are also decorated with a series of half-eyes and sectioned conch shells, both frequently seen motifs in Teotihuacan murals. All this influence from the past suggests that the Aztecs were amateur archaeologists themselves. Perhaps searching for their roots or simply curious about past cultures, they may have excavated in Teotihuacan and then, once back in their own capital city, tried to imitate what they had uncovered; they may have brought some of their finds, which would have been regarded as powerful supernatural objects, to the Great Temple to be placed in offertory caches.

The discovery of the Olmec maskette may have a different explanation. The Olmecs were temporally and spatially far removed from the Aztecs. Perhaps the piece was casually discovered by a farmer in the Olmec region, and then delivered as part of a tribute payment to Tenochtitlan. On the other hand, it may have been a treasured heirloom, handed down from generation to generation, and finally paid in tribute or given as a political gift to the Aztecs. Although we will never really know how the Aztecs viewed these objects, it is evident that they held the past in high regard, venerating and respecting their predecessors.

Faunal remains from offertory caches

Animal bones and other remains were found deposited alongside the man-made artifacts discussed above. The complete analysis of these remains is still being conducted by the Department of Prehistory of the Mexican Institute of Anthropology. It is, however, already possible to say something about those materials which have been studied and identified, especially those from offering 7, located on the southern side of the Great Temple. Based on these preliminary results, it is interesting to note that the majority of the animals identified were not native to the local environment of Tenochtitlan and the central highlands, but rather were brought from distant areas, especially the Atlantic and Pacific coasts. The quantity of faunal remains in caches suggests that they were an important component of offertory ritual at the Great Temple.

Many natural treasures came from the sea, and various types of shell in fact constitute the majority of invertebrate remains from offering 7. Most of the shells derive from coastal saltwater habitats, although some are from freshwater sources in central Mexico. To date, approximately 82 per cent of these saltwater shells have been identified, and most come from the

61–65

83

102

100

103

Gulf Coast region. Numerous specimens of conch shell were found, which is not surprising because these were commonly used in rituals as trumpets. Two were more specifically identified as the species *Strombus gigas*, native to the Atlantic coast. Clam shells and other species were also deposited. Various kinds of coral, many of the type commonly called brain coral, were also brought from coastal environments. Four sea urchins from the Pacific coast region were recovered: these creatures attach themselves to rocks, from which they can easily be removed. All the faunal remains are still in excellent condition, and must have been placed in the caches with great care.[16]

Offering 7 also yielded abundant fish remains. Many sawfish were found; these come from both the Atlantic and the Pacific Oceans. Skeletons of barracuda (*Sphyraena barracuda*), red snapper (*Lujtanus sp.*), "hen fish" (*Pomacanthus*), "parrot fish" (*Sparisoma*), and globefish (*Diodon*) were also excavated. Most of the Gulf Coast species are types that are easily captured in shallow waters with rocky or coral-reefed bottoms.[17] Similar finds to those of offering 7 were unearthed in offering 58.

Two major types of aquatic reptiles – turtles and crocodiles – predominated in offering 7. Altogether, seventy-three carapaces were identified, with specimens native to both coasts. Forty were of the *Kinosternon* family, most of these coming from sources in the Valley of Mexico; the remainder were from the Gulf Coast region between what is now central Veracruz and Campeche. Most of the marine fauna was captured in regions under Aztec control. Two crocodile heads were found, and may be the result of agricultural fertility rites. The Aztecs viewed the earth as an enormous monster called *cipactli*. The closest living thing to this creature may have been the sawfish, but was more probably the crocodile, which was perhaps also an earth symbol. There appears to have been some process of selection in determining which parts of the body were deposited in offerings. Turtles are represented by their shell alone while the heads and skins – but not the entire skeleton – of crocodiles were interred.

Snakes were also deposited in offertory caches, but only as skins attached to the skull; no vertebrae from below the cranium were found. Most specimens are rattlesnakes, a species abundant in the central highlands. At least fifteen rattlesnakes (*Crotalus*) were found in offering 7. Other identifiable snakes include the boa constrictor, from tropical coastal environments, and the fer de lance (*Bothrops atrox*), also from tropical habitats.

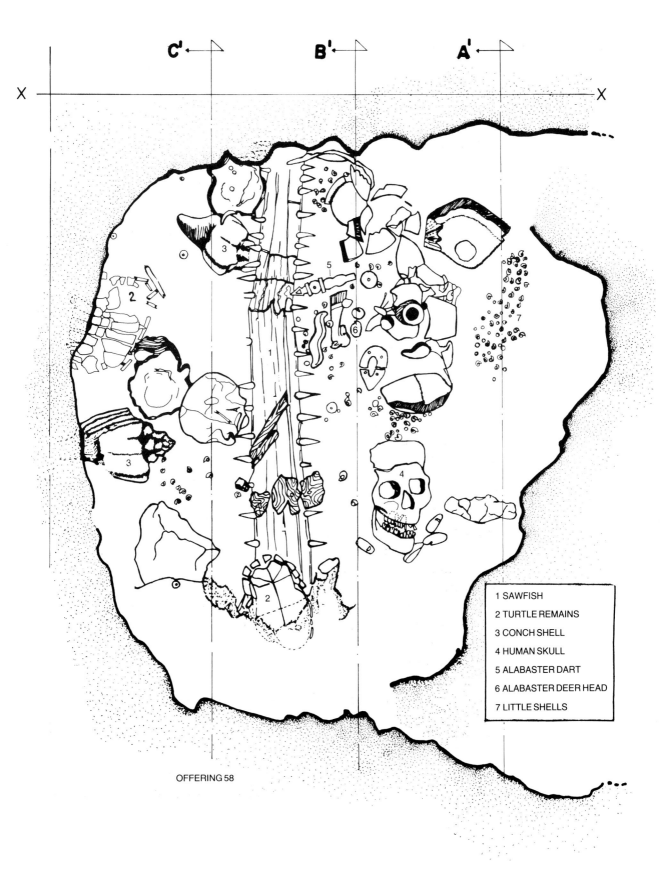

C' B' A'

X X

1 SAWFISH
2 TURTLE REMAINS
3 CONCH SHELL
4 HUMAN SKULL
5 ALABASTER DART
6 ALABASTER DEER HEAD
7 LITTLE SHELLS

OFFERING 58

100 Offering 58, the contents of which are similar to those in offering 7 (ills. 61–65).

Bird remains in offering 7 were relatively scarce. Only a few bird bone implements and four complete quail skeletons were found in this deposit.[18] This contrasts with the chronicles which mention birds as among the most common offerings to the gods.[19] Quails were frequently sacrificed in prehispanic ritual, and their blood sprinkled on the ground. Even today in rural areas, chickens or turkeys – substituting for quail – are sacrificed, and their blood offered to the earth in rites of agricultural fertility. Yet it appears that what was regarded as proper for sacrifice was not necessarily deemed appropriate for interment in offertory caches, for the chroniclers do not mention sea creatures, so abundant in caches, as common offerings.

All animals had special symbolism in prehispanic Mexico, and their presence in these offerings was not arbitrary[20], as is shown, for example, *101, V* by the skeleton of a jaguar with a greenstone ball in its jaws, from Chamber II. The careful arrangement of fauna within a cache and the selection of particular body parts suggest a certain order. Each creature was deposited in relation to the god honored in the cache. Specific placement was determined by the directional orientation of the offering, its relation to other objects around it, its depth in the ground, and other factors which cannot yet be fully interpreted.[21] When the analysis of faunal remains for all the Great Temple caches is complete, perhaps we will be able to define more clearly the motivations underlying specific placement of animals.

Concluding remarks

Although all the material excavated at the Great Temple is still in the process of analysis, it appears that the majority of artifacts represent or refer to Tlaloc, god of rain and earth. Many artifacts – such as ceramic and stone vessels, stone masks and figurines – depict the god himself. The abundance of marine fauna with aquatic connotations is perhaps also symbolic of this deity: remains of fish, shells, crocodiles, coral, and turtles can be linked to Tlaloc. In addition, small-scale stone representations of *118, 119* canoes, oars, and fish may have a similar significance, alluding to Tlaloc and his watery domain.

Many objects, however, are connected with Huitzilopochtli. No statues of this god are known to exist, but the chroniclers record that his image was made of amaranth dough and seeds.[22] Symbols referring to Huitzilopochtli are abundant. Braziers adorned with knotted bows, skulls of decapitated victims, sacrificial knives with mosaic eyes and teeth, and the quantity of objects from tribute-paying regions all allude to

Faunal remains from offerings

101 (top left) *Skull of a jaguar with a large greenstone ball in its jaws, from Chamber II, in the Stage IV Temple. The presence of the greenstone may refer to the myth of the jaguar which was waiting to devour the spirit of the deceased at the end of nine trials in the underworld, but was given a jade bead in place of the deceased's heart.*

102 (top right) *Coral appeared often among the offerings.*

103 (above) *Crocodile skull. The crocodile, an aquatic reptile, was associated with Tlaloc.*

104 (right) *Shell with greenstone beads inside. Offering 41, Stage IVb.*

Huitzilopochtli, the ultimate deity of war and tribute, and the god most closely identified with the Aztec state.

The ritually deposited materials described in this chapter constitute a metaphoric language signifying the most fundamental needs of the Aztecs, as discussed in Chapter 2: agriculture and warfare. Aztec culture was completely dependent on manifestations of this dichotomy; food and tribute, water and fire (a metaphor for war), and life and death in sacrifice, were all essential for Aztec survival. These concerns are present in the symbolism of the Great Temple of Tenochtitlan and are given mythological justification, for the Aztecs viewed conquests as their rightful duty – just as Huitzilopochtli conquered his brothers and his sister Coyolxauhqui, and then appropriated their *anecuyotl*, or destiny. Symbolically this is important because, in this way, the Aztecs continued the mission begun by their tutelary god; they not only took charge of the destiny of those whom they had conquered, but they also appropriated the fruits of their production, both agricultural and artistic. Massive quantities of maize, *chía*, and amaranth arrived at Tenochtitlan, as well as cotton mantles, cured animal skins, and featherwork warrior costumes and insignia.

The significance of the offerings from the Great Temple is evident in these words of Diego Durán:

When Motecusoma [Motecuhzoma I] observed the speed with which his temple [the Great Temple] was built, he sent word to all the lords of the land that, in order that his god [Huitzilopochtli] be the most honored, the most revered, they should collect in all the cities a great quantity of precious stones, of green jade – which they call *chalchihuitl* – and clear transparent ones, and blood stones, emeralds, rubies, and carnelian. That is, every kind of rich stone and jewel. And so it was that each city, striving to surpass the others, arrived with its jewels and precious stones to throw them into the foundations, each one in turn, in such a way that they threw in so many rich stones, so much treasure, that it was an astonishing thing; and they said that their god [Huitzilopochtli] had given them those riches, so it was appropriate that they be dedicated to his service, since they truly belonged to him.[23]

All the above – the actual riches discovered in the Great Temple and the descriptions of the chroniclers – indicate that both the vestiges of ancient cultures and the wealth of contemporary peoples controlled by the Aztecs were interred in the Great Temple in honor of Tlaloc and Huitzilopochtli.

This ritual and economic focus on the structure which constituted the ideological core of the Aztec empire served to exalt their military-political control over the land, and strengthened the idea that their Temple was the true center of the universe. The Aztecs demonstrated that they were the chosen people of the gods and that order in the universe was dependent upon their sovereignty.

CHAPTER FIVE

AZTEC MYTH AND
THE GREAT TEMPLE

Numerous studies have been dedicated to the Aztec conception of the
universe, often revealed by their myths. This structured way of viewing the
heavenly bodies and the earth, as well as the placement of the gods and of
man himself in the cosmos, forms part of their complex philosophy and
religion, their worldview.

The structure of the Aztec universe consists basically of three levels: the
highest or celestial level; the central or terrestrial tier; and the lowest level
or the underworld. The upper and lower levels are further subdivided and
will be treated in greater detail below.

The theory proposed here is that in the Aztec mind, the celestial and
subterrestrial levels (realms of the vertical dimension) intersect the
terrestrial tier (the horizontal median) at a central point where the Great
Temple of Tenochtitlan stands; thus the Temple represents the Aztec
conception of the universe in symbolic form, a material crystallization of
some of their principal myths. The organization of the Great Temple, its
architectural plan, sculptures, and offerings, as well as its location within
the capital of Tenochtitlan, all contribute to the symbolic impact of the
Temple as the ultimate manifestation of Aztec philosophy and religion.

The celestial level

This realm is formed of thirteen "heavens" or skies, although some
sources speak of nine or twelve. The gods live in the ninth heaven and
above. Nine heavens are mentioned by the midwife immediately after a
baby has been born and is being washed:

105 Reconstruction of an Aztec pyramid-temple at Santa Cecelia, northwest of Mexico City.

Merciful lady . . . your servant has arrived, he who has been sent here by our mother, our father, Ometecuhtli and Omecihuatl, who live in the ninth heaven, in the place where these gods dwell.[1]

107   Prehispanic peoples' beliefs in these different heavens probably resulted from observation of the movement of celestial bodies. The Codex Vaticanus A 3738 illustrates the thirteen-level scheme of the celestial realm with reference to specific heavenly bodies. The first or lowest of these heavens is the place where the moon and clouds are found, and these can be seen by everyone. The stars lie in the second heaven, known as the Citlalco, "Place of stars." Stars are divided into two large groups: those in the north are the Centzon Mimixcoa, "the innumerable ones of the north," and the Centzon Huitznahua are "the innumerable ones of the south." From the third heaven the sun leaves each day to cross the sky, and in the fourth heaven is the planet Venus or, according to some sources, Uixtocihuatl, the goddess of salt waters, sister of the water deities, the Tlaloques.[2] Comets occupy the fifth heaven, which is considered to be the "rotating heaven." The following two skies or heavens are represented only by colors, green and blue or blue and black. In the eighth heaven tempests are said to form. This is the Iztapalnacazcayan, "Place where the corners are of obsidian blades." The gods dwell in the following three heavens; and the last two, the twelfth and thirteenth, constitute the highest levels, known as Omeyocan, the "Place of duality."[3]

The terrestrial level

From the center of this level radiate the four world directions. Each one is identified with a creator god, a specific calendrical symbol and a color which varies according to different historical versions.

East corresponds to the deity Red Tezcatlipoca and is called Tlapallan, "Place of [red] color;" its symbol is a reed. North is associated with the Black Tezcatlipoca and is the region called Mictlampa, "Place of death;" its associated symbol is a flint knife. South corresponds to the Blue Tezcatlipoca, who is actually Huitzilopochtli, solar god and war deity. This is the Huitztlampa, "Region of thorns," the symbol of which is the

XV *Olmec maskette of green jade, dated to 800 BC, the oldest object found in the Great Temple excavations. Stage IV, AD 1454, offering 20. Ht 10.5 cm.*

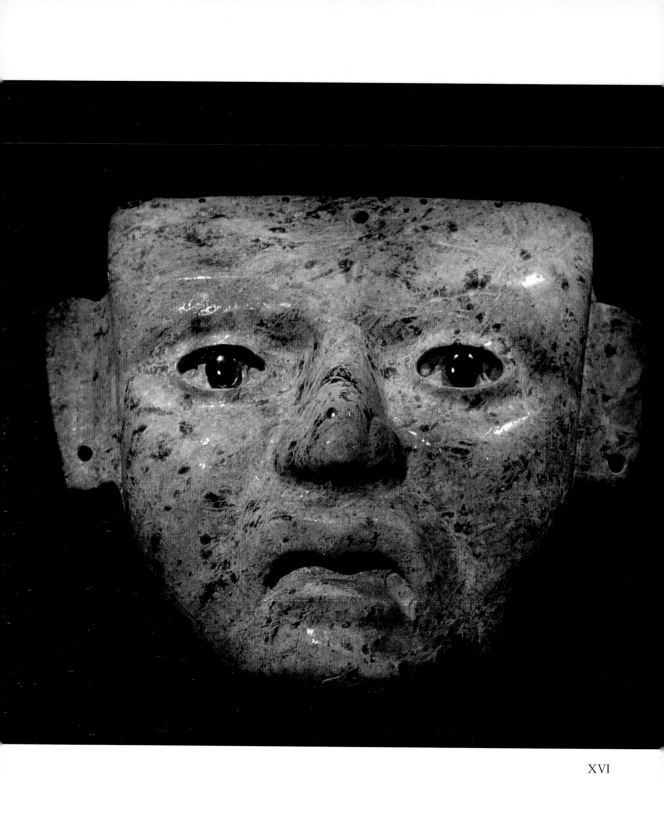

XVI

rabbit. In the west, where the sun goes down into the land of night and the dead, Ehecatl-Quetzalcoatl, God of Wind, is found. Called Cihuatlampa, "Place of women," it was to the west that the Cihuateteo, deified women who had died in childbirth, escorted the sun each evening after his journey across the sky. The west's color is white and its symbol a house.

Each of the four directions is also identified with a certain plant, as can be seen in the Codex Féjérvary-Mayer, a prehispanic ritual-divinatory manuscript. The function of each plant or tree is to hold up the sky. In addition, together with the central axis or cosmic tree, they form a conduit by which the sacred energies of the gods can descend to the earth.[4]

The conceptual pivot where these four directions intersected with the vertical channel that led upward to the celestial tiers, and down to the underworld, was the spot where the Great Temple was built, a very sacred location. Sacred space referred to special areas made holy because of their role in facilitating communication with the gods. The Aztecs quite clearly considered there to be a hierarchy of such divine space. An example from one end of the scale could be a small shrine dedicated to Tezcatlipoca and set up at a crossroads. At the other extreme, however, the ultimate sacred space was the great ceremonial precinct in the center of Tenochtitlan.

Adding greater emphasis to this symbolism, the city was constructed in the middle of a lake; it was sometimes called Cemanahuac, "Place in a circle of water," envisioned as a great turquoise ring. The Aztecs' homeland, Aztlan, was also located in the middle of a lake. By extension, all shores and the sea – which could also be called Cemanahuac – recalled the layout of Aztlan, with a core of land surrounded by a ring of water. By claiming to be situated at the center of the universe, the Aztecs could project the message that they were the chosen people.

106

It was from the struggles of cosmic forces released by the gods of the four directions that the process of transformation began, resulting in the creation of the four suns or ages, and of humankind which lives in the terrestrial realm. This mythological model posits the eternal dialectic as the force that ensures continuation of the cosmos. Universal equilibrium is maintained because of the never-ending battle between opposing forces; thus, conflict and competition are important values which maintain social and political balance.

XVI *Greenstone Teotihuacan-style mask with obsidian eyes. Stage IV Temple, offering 20. Ht 20 cm.*

106 The city of Tenochtitlan, drawn by conquistador Anónimo.

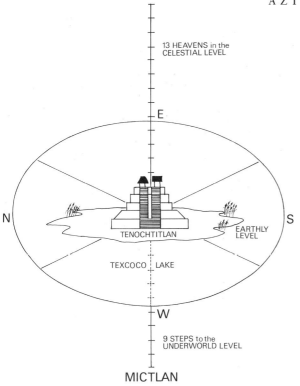

OMEYOCAN

13 HEAVENS in the
CELESTIAL LEVEL

E

N

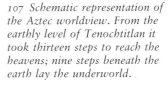

TENOCHTITLAN

EARTHLY
LEVEL

S

TEXCOCO LAKE

W

9 STEPS to the
UNDERWORLD LEVEL

MICTLAN

107 Schematic representation of the Aztec worldview. From the earthly level of Tenochtitlan it took thirteen steps to reach the heavens; nine steps beneath the earth lay the underworld.

The underworld

Just as there are thirteen heavens (or sometimes nine, or twelve), so there are nine subterrestrial levels through which the deceased must pass before reaching the underworld, Mictlan, "Land of the Dead," also called Chiconamictlan, "Ninth place of the dead," and according to Sahagún the abode of the gods of death.

107

The Codex Vaticanus A 3738 records these nine levels as: the earth, the path through water, the place where hills are found, the hill of obsidian, the place of winds formed by obsidian knives, the place where flags wave, the place where people are shot with arrows and where hearts are eaten, the "Obsidian place of the dead," and the place where no opening exists for smoke to escape.[5] Sahagún offered a different description of some of these regions: where two hills clashed together, where a great serpent stood guard over the road, the place of the green lizard, the place of eight barren plateaux and eight mountain passes where the cold wind was made of sharp knives, and, finally, where the deceased had to cross the Chiconahuapan River on the back of a dog to reach Mictlan.[6]

Why were there nine stages to reach the other world? Various authors have suggested different reasons: that death is related to night and in the prehispanic calendar there were nine "Lords of night;" that a week in ancient times had nine days;[7] or that a day was made up of nine time-periods.[8] My theory is quite different: the nine steps followed by someone who dies a natural death represent the reversal of the gestation period, a return to the maternal womb – which is the earth – from which life sprang. In Aztec thought the celestial levels are masculine, since from these flow heat and rain, or divine semen, while the earth, which receives this fertilization, is feminine, and within her the plants grow.

The Aztecs knew that menstruation ceases for nine occasions when a woman is pregnant, and that at the end of this time the child is born. But just before birth, water is released from the womb. The uterus is a dark cave, with no light, just as Mictlan is described. It is not surprising, therefore, that the Aztecs arranged a dead person's body in a fetal position, with legs drawn up, and sprinkled water on the corpse. In this way an individual might return to the same position and environment as in the womb.

Furthermore, in ancient Aztec mythology, the cave – the uterus of the earth – gives birth to individuals and to entire ethnic groups. The walls of caves in pictorial documents are portrayed in the same way as human skin, with a rough yellowish finish. Chicomoztoc, the Seven Caves from which the Aztecs emerged, is represented in the *Historia Tolteca-Chichimeca*,[9] and other ancient manuscripts, as a womb. Scholars studying this *Historia* explain that the Caves open to release humanity, just as the womb gives forth the newborn child.[10] The practice of placing the remains of some individuals in large jars may also be considered a return to the womb, to the original cave.[11]

In conclusion, darkness, water, and the flexed position of the deceased, all relate to the Aztecs' anatomical and physiological knowledge, and are metaphorically associated with life and death. The phenomenon that holds back the flow of blood for nine occasions and at the end of this period produces life, can be seen inversely in the need to follow the nine steps to return to the great womb of the earth.

The Temple as an expression of the Aztec worldview

As we have seen, the Great Temple is a microcosm of the Aztec vision of the world, in which both horizontal and vertical dimensions have special cosmic significance. In my view, the platform supporting the Temple corresponds to the terrestrial level; this interpretation is reinforced by the sculptures of serpents – symbols of the earth – located upon it. Two large braziers stand on either side of the serpent-head sculptures, at the center of

109

Serpent sculptures

108 (above) *An undulating stone serpent at the southern end of the Stage IVb Temple platform, on the side dedicated to Huitzilopochtli.*

109 (right) *Serpent altar and braziers on the south side of the Stage IV Temple structure. The bows or knots on the braziers are symbolic of the war god, Huitzilopochtli.*
Ht of braziers, 1.2 m.

110 (overleaf) *An artist's reconstruction drawing (made before the recent excavations) of the Great Temple precinct at Tenochtitlan.*

the north and south façades, and on the east side on an axis with the central line of the Tlaloc and Huitzilopochtli shrines. These braziers indicate that it was on the platform, which signified the earthly level, that ephemeral offerings were usually made.

The celestial levels are represented by the four slightly tapering tiers of the pyramid which rise to the summit where stand the two shrines of the principal gods, the supreme level: Omeyocan or "Place of duality."

The lower levels, corresponding to the underworld, are below the earthly platform. The majority of the offerings – many durable but some perishable – have been found beneath this great floor.

The words addressed to Ahuitzotl, Aztec ruler from 1486 to 1502, by Nezahualpilli, ruler of Texcoco, during the festivities to celebrate the completion of one of the construction stages of the Great Temple, reflect this belief in a sacred center:

Although you are very young, because you are the sovereign of such a powerful kingdom, which is the root, the navel and the heart of this entire worldly apparatus, make it your destiny to see that the honor of the Aztecs does not diminish but rather becomes greater.[12]

In vertical terms, the Great Temple is formed of two halves, representing two sacred mountains. The southern half signifies Coatepec Hill, where Huitzilopochtli defeated his opponents, while the northern side represents the "Hill of sustenance," Tonacatepetl, where Tlaloc was patron deity. These two hills or shrines may also symbolize one of the places – where two mountains crashed together and crushed the traveler – through which the deceased passed on the way to Mictlan, according to Sahagún's account.

The use of a temple to signify an ideal model of universal order and a central point where all levels intersect – the *axis mundi* – is not restricted to the Great Temple of the Aztecs, but is found in many other religions. Mircea Eliade, a specialist in comparative religions, states:

All these sacred constructions symbolically represent the whole universe: the floors or terraces are identified with the "heavens" or cosmic levels. In one sense, each one reproduces the cosmic mountain, that is, it is considered to have been built in the "center of the world."[13]
... because they are situated in the center of the cosmos, the temple or the sacred city always constitute the point where the three cosmic regions meet.[14]

The entire ceremonial precinct of Tenochtitlan with its seventy-eight structures, described by Sahagún, is also closely related to the Aztec worldview. The placement of each building was significant, often with reference to the Great Temple in the center, and conformed to the Aztec conception of its role within space and time in the universe. Examples are the Temple of the Sun, situated toward the southwest corner of the precinct, and the temple of Tezcatlipoca, powerful god of Fate, which lay to the south of the Great Temple. Another example is the temple of Ehecatl-Quetzalcoatl, "God of winds preceding the rains," located, according to the chronicles, in front of the Great Temple. A temple dedicated to this god was placed in a similar position in neighboring Tlatelolco. Perhaps this orientation is related to the myth of the creation of the Fifth Sun at Teotihuacan. According to this myth, all the gods gathered to see from which direction the sun would rise, each facing one of the four cardinal directions. Ehecatl faced east, and it was from here that the sun rose: therefore the temple of Ehecatl-Quetzalcoatl in the ceremonial precinct has its main façade toward the east.

Myths symbolized by the Great Temple

As we saw in Chapter 2, myths may be used to resolve theological questions, man creating gods in his own image. The symbolic components of the Aztec Great Temple re-enact their myths in the form of ritual. Let us now examine the archaeology of the Temple in relation to those myths of which we have knowledge from sixteenth-century chronicles.

In prehispanic times, images and their location within a sacred structure communicated multi-dimensional messages with mythological, religious, philosophical, and political meanings. We know that the Great Temple represents two mountains, Coatepec on Huitzilopochtli's side and the "Hill of sustenance" on the half dedicated to Tlaloc. Francisco del Paso y Troncoso and Miguel León-Portilla[15] have already commented on the Temple's association with Coatepec, but I would like to add some observations of my own. Huitzilopochtli's side possesses several archaeological features that recall the myth of the war god's birth and his subsequent struggle with his sister, Coyolxauhqui, on Coatepec Hill. These can be summarized as follows:

—Myth records that after his victory, Huitzilopochtli remained on top of Coatepec. His shrine, on the summit of the Temple pyramid, occupies a similar position. No images of Huitzilopochtli are known to have survived, but chroniclers such as Bernal Díaz[16] and Diego Durán described this deity's statue inside the shrine, as we saw in Chapter 3.

30 —In the same myth Coyolxauhqui was decapitated by her brother, and her body was dismembered by being thrown to the bottom of the hill.[17] The enormous bas-relief sculpture discovered at the Great Temple represents the goddess in her decapitated and dismembered state. This sculpture was found on the platform at the base of the Temple, on the earthly level at the foot of the pyramidal "hill" from which Coyolxauhqui was cast after her defeat.

—Coyolxauhqui images occur in a number of the building stages of the Great Temple, suggesting a continuity of this symbolism through time. The monumental relief carving of the goddess was found at the Stage IVb level; another similar relief sculpture was located directly below this, on the Stage IV platform. A stone fragment of part of the face of a Coyolxauhqui, very similar to that from Stage IVb, was unearthed during the excavations and may be associated with a later stage. The huge, three-dimensional diorite head of Coyolxauhqui, now in the National Museum of Anthropology, is also known to have come from this area, but its exact provenience is unrecorded.

—Decapitated female skulls were found in offerings associated with the Stage IVb Coyolxauhqui sculpture. Sacrifice by decapitation was principally carried out in rites involving female victims, but in this case such rituals may have been related to a re-enactment of the myth of Huitzilopochtli's victory over Coyolxauhqui.

36 —The sacrificial stone at the entrance to Huitzilopochtli's shrine perhaps refers to the immolation of his sister and may have been used in rites recreating the mythical event.

—In Construction Stage II, a sculpted face set into the top step may represent Cuicatlicac. It will be remembered that, according to myth, Cuicatlicac warned Huitzilopochtli of the progress of his brothers, the Huitznahua, as they made their way toward Coatepec Hill. Alternatively, the face could represent Painal, a god often associated with Huitzilopochtli, although it is more likely that his statue would have been placed in the shrine itself.

108, 109 —Representations of serpents abound at the Great Temple and perhaps also allude to the name Coatepec, "Serpent Hill."

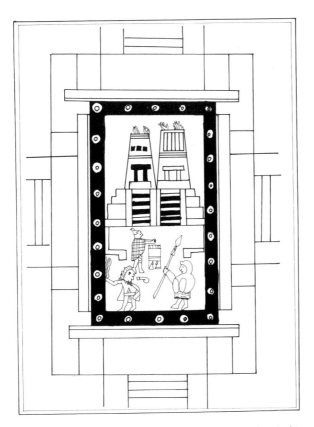

III Sacred space: the Great Temple precinct. Codex Aubin.

—Some undecorated stones protrude from the surface of the Temple body at Stage III level, on the side dedicated to Huitzilopochtli. Perhaps they are an attempt to symbolize a hill; hills and mountains are represented by similar protuberances in the pictorial codices.

—Some of the statues found reclining against the stairway of Stage III may represent the Centzon Huitznahua, Huitzilopochtli's defeated brothers.

112, 113

IX

As well as the above archaeological evidence, further insight into how the Temple may have been used to recreate the Huitzilopochtli myth – by symbolizing the mountain and providing a stage for the re-enactment of dramatic rites – may be gleaned from the chronicles and pictorial codices.

Perhaps the clearest account of the temple-mountain relationship is found in the description of the elaborate rites conducted at the Great Temple during the festival of Panquetzaliztli. This celebration, dedicated to Huitzilopochtli, was one of the principal occasions for the collection of tribute and was an important state event. Several aspects of these rites

112, 113 *Stone sculptures, originally covered by the fill of later construction stages, found reclining against the stairway of the Stage III Temple. It is thought the figures may represent Huitzilopochtli's mythical brothers, the Huitznahua, who fought a battle with him on Coatepec Hill.*

suggest that the Temple was viewed as a specific sacred hill, where the myth of Coyolxauhqui's defeat could be recreated.

According to Sahagún, during this festival sacrificial slaves bearing gifts of men's mantles and women's garments walked to the Temple; this may recall the Aztec pilgrimage to Coatepec. Then two groups of slaves – one from the Huitznahua *barrio* – engaged in a mock battle, probably re-enacting the confrontation between Huitzilopochtli and his four hundred brothers. Captives representing these Huitznahua, who – in myth – fled from the war god around Coatepec Hill, were then led in procession around the Temple and sacrificed in the Huitznahua temple. Their bodies were rolled down the Temple steps to arrive mutilated at the bottom, perhaps again recalling the fate of Coyolxauhqui.

18 Serpents were also prominent at the Panquetzaliztli ceremony. The mythological Fire Serpent, *xiuhcoatl*, which was also Huitzilopochtli's magic weapon, was imitated by a paper serpent with red feathers – representing fire – emerging from its gaping jaws. Torches were also used to symbolize the Fire Serpent, and there was a serpent dance.

Allusions to the Coyolxauhqui myth are found in other annual rites, sometimes subtle – involving interpretation of ritual acts – but often more direct, as, for example, during the month of Toxcatl and the feast in honor of the god Tezcatlipoca, where an image of Huitzilopochtli was made of amaranth-seed dough and placed on a figurative hill of serpents in the Huitznahua temple. Sahagún describes the ceremony:

In the temple called Huitznahuac they made a wooden . . . bench . . . carved in the form of serpents . . . For the [god's] image, the bones were made of mesquite wood, which were then covered with dough until the figure of a man was formed.[18]

Perhaps the most significant aspect of the dough image was its garments:

Before the figure of the god . . . were piled bones made of amaranth dough, and these were covered with the same mantle that covered the image. This was adorned with designs of bones and parts of the body of a dismembered person.[19]

It may be that the limbs decorating the cape are yet another reference to the dismemberment of Coyolxauhqui.

Again, probable references to the Coyolxauhqui myth occurred during the festival of Ochpaniztli, "Sweeping of the way," which honored the mother of the gods, Coatlicue, also called Toci. Durán describes how the goddess was personified by a woman carrying a broom, thus re-enacting at

114 Huitzilopochtli in his temple. Codex Azcatitlan.

the Temple the scene on Coatepec Hill where Coatlicue became pregnant with Huitzilopochtli. The impersonator was taken to the summit of the Great Temple and decapitated. Her corpse was then flayed and her skin donned by a man, perhaps a priest, who became her surrogate:

Thus arrayed, the man . . . was taken out before . . . those Huaxtecs [who were] all dressed and armed for war. While they left through the Temple doors, all the nobles and leading men of the city entered through the courtyard gates . . . well armed with their swords and shields . . . and . . . they feigned a skirmish.[20]

Later, during the same festival, some of the sacrificial victims were taken to the top of a scaffold, thrown to the ground, and then beheaded. Such ritual acts of battles and of sacrifice by being thrown from a height and then decapitated within the setting of the Great Temple are yet further suggestions of the mythical events of Coatepec Hill. Most of the sacrificial victims during the feast of Panquetzaliztli were war captives, just as Coyolxauhqui had herself been held captive by her brother.

The Codex Azcatitlan provides even further evidence for the temple-mountain relationship. Within this codex is depicted a hill – "Couatep" – with four serpents emerging from it. On the summit stands a temple, surmounted by Huitzilopochtli wearing a hummingbird disguise and holding a spear and shields. Another temple is drawn in front of the first, with a serpent emerging from it and bearing a standard on its back; above this second temple are written the words *xiuhcohual oncatemoc*. Clearly the mountain and serpents form a glyph for Coatepec, with Huitzilopochtli standing above, armed and ready for battle. *Xiuhcohual* (that is, *xiuhcoatl*) indicates Huitzilopochtli's magic Fire-Serpent weapon, while *oncatemoc* (meaning "place where he descended") is a reference to its appearance. The symbolic meaning of the whole is that the invincible arms of Huitzilopochtli descend on Coatepec Hill to vanquish all enemies.[21]

114

The northern side of the Great Temple, dedicated to Tlaloc, also seems to symbolize a mountain. We know that Tlaloc was patron of the earth's fertility, a provider of food through his fructifying waters which often formed in clouds on mountain tops. This belief is seen in many of the rites held in his honor at the summit of hills. Durán[22] describes splendid ceremonies specially dedicated to this god, held on a hill near the present-day city of Puebla, today called Mount Tlaloc but in prehispanic times known as Tlalocan, "Place of Tlaloc." Over a period of a number of days all the rulers and nobles of Central Mexico made rich offerings at a shrine on the mountain top. These consisted of jewels and other valuable objects, but mainly they were all types of food, representing the gifts given to humankind by Tlaloc, on his hill, a hill of sustenance.

In my view another Nahua myth is associated with Tlaloc's side of the Great Temple. This myth explains how man got food from the gods. It takes place at Tonacatepetl, the "Hill of sustenance," where red ants hoarded maize kernels, the basis for human subsistence. According to the version rendered in the *Leyenda de los Soles* (Legend of the Suns):

Again they said, "What are you saying, O gods? Now all are searching for food." Then the ant went for maize kernels within the Tonacatepetl. Quetzalcoatl met the ant and asked it, "Tell me where you get [the maize]." Many times he asked, but it refused to answer. Finally [the ant] said, "Over there" [and pointed to the place]. Then Quetzalcoatl . . . transformed himself into a black ant and went with it; they entered [the hill] and together carried out [the maize] . . . to Tamoanchan. The gods chewed it and then placed it in our [human] mouths to strengthen us.

XVII *Necklace made of figures carved in mother-of-pearl, representing frogs, serpent heads, and rattles. Found in Chamber II, Stage IV Temple. Ht of figures 1–5.7 cm.*

XVIII *Silver maskette representing a skeletal face with three bells on the chin; serpents form the ear ornaments. Found inside an obsidian funerary urn in offering 34 (see ills. 94, 95). Ht 4.9 cm.*

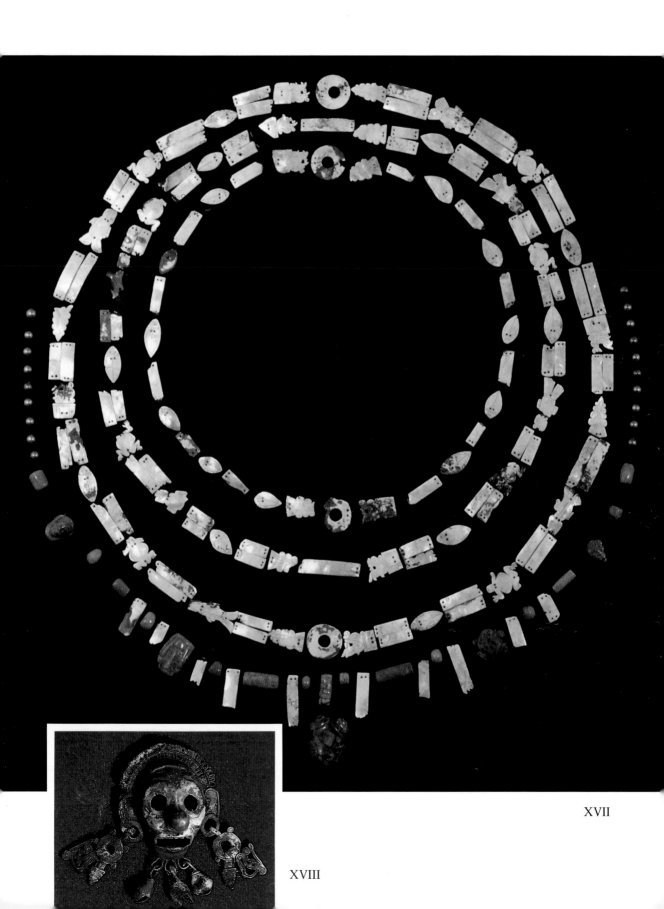

XVII

XVIII

Then they said, "What shall we do with the Tonacatepetl?" Quetzalcoatl went alone [to the mountain], he tied it with ropes and tried to carry it off on his back, but he could not lift it.

Then Oxomoco cast lots with the maize kernels, and Cipactonal, Oxomoco's wife, also used the kernels to tell the future . . . Oxomoco and Cipactonal said that only Nanahuatl ["the one with pustules," an aspect of Quetzalcoatl], could remove the maize from the Tonacatepetl, by attacking it with a club, because he had discovered it. All the Tlaloques [gods of rain], were advised: the blue Tlaloques, the white Tlaloques, the yellow Tlaloques, and the red Tlaloques. And Nanahuatzin [honorific for Nanahuatl] attacked [the hill] with blows and thus got out the maize. But then the Tlaloques seized all the food: the white, black [or blue], yellow, and red maize, beans, amaranth, *chía* [a type of sage], *michihuauhtli* ["fish" amaranth]; all the food was snatched away [by the Tlaloques].[23]

This important myth tells us that it was on a *hill* that Quetzalcoatl discovered maize; he then took it to the home of the gods, Tamoanchan, so they could give it to men as the basic foodstuff. But then the Tlaloques, whose colors may represent the world directions, or perhaps the colors of maize, seized all the food. However, Tlaloc and his assistants the Tlaloques did provide food for men and animals because they, as rain gods, fertilize the earth and make the plants grow.

To end this chapter I want to emphasize the sacred character of the hill as the Tonacatepetl, "Hill of sustenance." This same sacred character is seen in the temple-hill of Tlaloc in the Great Temple, and is represented also in the Codex Borbonicus.

In conclusion, it can be seen that archaeological data together with information from historical sources help us interpret the symbolism of the Great Temple. Not only was this temple the *axis mundi*, the navel of the Aztec universe, but it was the place where some of the main myths came alive, re-enacted through ritual. Tlaloc and Huitzilopochtli are joined in architecture, in myth and in ritual, and these two gods represent water and war, life and death, food and tribute, all fundamental to the very existence of the Aztec people.

XIX (above left) *Stone pendant in the form of a god's face. Stage IV, Chamber II. Ht 8 cm.*

XX (above right) *Head of a deer carved in alabaster, one of many found in caches during the excavation. Ht 10 cm.*

XXI–XXIII (below) *Ceremonial knives inlaid with shell, imitating faces in profile. Average ht 10 cm.*

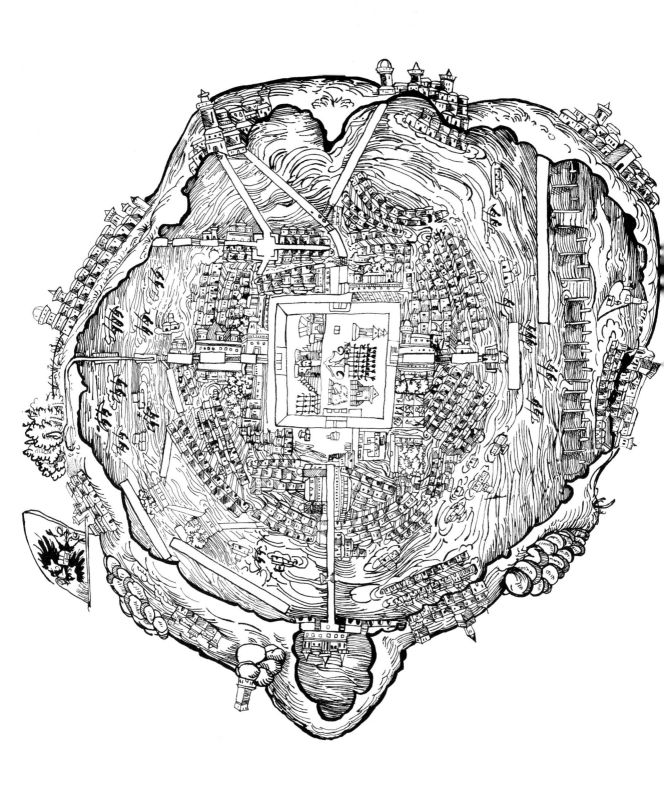

CHAPTER SIX

TENOCHTITLAN AND
ITS INHABITANTS

What can the sixteenth-century chronicles tell us about Tenochtitlan, the lives of its inhabitants, and the eventual demise of the city?

And when we beheld so many cities and towns on the water, and other large settlements built on firm ground, and that broad causeway running so straight and perfectly level to the city of Tenochtitlan, we were astonished, and we said that it was like the things of enchantment we had read of in the book of Amadis of Gaul, because of the great towers and temples and buildings that rose up out of the water, and all were made of stone masonry. Some of our soldiers said that all these things seemed to be a dream; and it is no wonder that I write here in this manner, for there is much to ponder in this, and I do not know how to tell it, for never was there seen, nor heard, nor even dreamt, anything like that which we then observed.[1]

    These are Bernal Díaz del Castillo's first impressions of Aztec civilization when he first entered Tenochtitlan with Cortés and his men on 8 November 1519. At that time Motecuhzoma II was ruler, and initially he treated the Spanish most cordially, lodging them in his father's palace and proudly displaying to them, from the summit of the Great Temple (of Tlatelolco) the panoramic view of the lake and all its cities. Bernal Díaz continues:

Motecuhzoma then took [Cortés] by the hand and told him to observe his great city and all the other settlements that were built in the water, and many other towns constructed on firm land surrounding the lake. . . . And thus we saw it, for that tall but accursed Temple was so high that the whole scene could be commanded from here. From this point we could see the three causeways that connected Mexico with the mainland. . . . And we saw the aqueduct of

115 The city of Tenochtitlan, a view traditionally attributed to Hernán Cortés. Note the three main causeways running to the north, south, and west, the eastern causeway terminating at the lake. North is at the top.

116 Tlatelolco, sister city of Tenochtitlan, with the remains of the great pyramid which Cortés climbed. The church of Santiago de Tlatelolco now stands above it.

Chapultepec, which brought pure water into the city, and the drawbridges which allowed water from the lagoon to go from one side of the causeway to the other. . . . . We were amazed at the multitude of canoes in that great lake, some laden with foodstuffs, others with different kinds of wares and merchandise. . . . Each house in this great city and the houses in all the other cities built in the water were connected by small wooden drawbridges . . . or else [people used] canoes. . . . The temples and shrines were built in the form of towers and fortresses and were white-washed, which made them shine [like silver]. The houses had flat roofs [like terraces], and along the roads there were other towers and adoratories like fortresses. . . . We observed the large plaza and the great multitude of people there, some buying, some selling. The clamor and noise of the people in the marketplace could be heard more than a league away. Among us some soldiers who had been in different parts of the world, in Constantinople, in Rome, or in other places in Italy, said that they had never seen a marketplace so large, so well ordered, so well controlled, with such harmony and with so many people, as this one.[2]

120

Cortés, in his letters to the king of Spain, compared Tenochtitlan with the Spanish city of Sevilla, although he stated that the former was much larger and had more inhabitants. He also thought that the buildings of Tenochtitlan were very fine, and that this city was better supplied with birds, game, fish, vegetables, and bread.[3]

Examination of the nobles' palaces, the houses of the working class, and the public areas such as the city's great plazas, will help us to gain an idea of what urban life in Tenochtitlan was like. We may also learn how the labor force was organized for the construction of a large part of the city.

Houses and palaces

Even Hernán Cortés marveled at the luxurious residences of the Aztec nobles. He described the palace of the lord of Iztapalapa thus:

Some new houses . . . are as splendid as the finest in Spain . . . as large and as well built, referring to the stone work and the woodwork and the flooring, and there are quarters for every type of service necessary in the house. Except that certain kinds of stone masonry and other elaborate finishings that are found in the houses in Spain, are lacking here. On the upper stories as well as on the ground floor there are fine gardens, with many trees and flowers of pleasing scent. There are also fresh water pools, very well made, with stairs that lead down to the bottom. Next to the palace stands a large orchard, above which is built a pavilion with many handsome rooms and hallways. Within the orchard there is an enormous fresh water pool, all square, the walls made of fine masonry. Around this pool is a walkway, its floor well paved with large stones, that is so wide that four can walk abreast along it; and it has four hundred paces on each side, which make 1,600 all around. Within the pool are many fish and around it numerous birds, such as wild duck, garganey, and other aquatic fowl; there are so many that they almost completely cover the water. On the other side of the walkway, toward the wall of the orchard, grow clumps of reeds, and beyond these are woods and fragrant herbs.[4]

118, 119

If this was the palace of a ruler of only secondary importance, then the sumptuousness of the palace of Motecuhzoma must have been even more impressive. This latter building occupied the site where the present-day National Palace stands.

Bernal Díaz described Motecuhzoma's residence as having innumerable rooms. In the dining room there was a low wooden throne (*icpalli*), and a low table covered with fine cloths. A golden-colored wooden door screened the ruler while he ate, so that members of the palace could not observe him. He was served by many women and entertained by singers, musicians, dancers, and some hunchbacks who amused him.

An armory was maintained in one hall, and in another were kept the accounts of tribute paid to Tenochtitlan. Part of the palace housed a magnificent aviary filled with countless species of birds brought from both distant tropical lands and nearby regions. There was even a special pond for aquatic birds. Another area housed a zoo with animals such as jaguars, foxes, and snakes. Fearsome rattlesnakes were raised in large feather-filled bins where they laid their eggs. The palace also had special rooms where women wove textiles for the royal household, and workshops for different types of artisans. Bernal Díaz described the gardens and baths:

117

We must not forget the gardens filled with fragrant flowers and trees . . . and the harmony and beauty of the promenades, and the ponds with fresh water, and canals with running water, as well as the baths. . . . The trees are full of small birds that breed there and the gardens with medicinal plants so useful and curative that they are amazing. . . . The grounds are full of orchards and vegetable gardens and everything is made of fine cut stone, all plastered and polished; this is seen in the baths as well as in the courts and walkways and terraces, and in the halls destined for dining, as well as those designed for dancing and singing. There was so much to see and admire in these gardens, as in the rest of the palace, that we never ceased to wonder at the magnificence here.[5]

An entire corps of specialized personnel took care of all aspects of the palace, including its administration and the personal needs of Motecuhzoma. In turn these people had to be fed and maintained by state revenues, for as full-time retainers they were removed from the productive workforce.

In Aztec society the type of home in which a person lived was a clear indication of his status. The royal palaces and fine homes of the nobles were all built near the main square of the Great Temple, and then each *calpulli* or territorial unit had its own squares and temples on a smaller scale. The nobles' houses were made of stone and white-washed plaster. The interior walls were covered with stucco, made by mixing sand and lime with water, which formed a kind of white cement, and on which were

23, 24 painted murals of vivid colors. The *macehualtin* (potters, stonecutters, jewelers, weavers, and even farmers and fishermen) inhabited humbler dwellings in the different *calpultin*. Their houses were made of wattle and daub, or of adobe bricks formed of mud mixed with material such as straw or rushes, to give it a better consistency. Straw and wood were also used in the construction of houses, and especially the sloping gabled roofs.

117 Stone sculpture of a rattlesnake from offering 41. L. 17.4 cm.

118, 119 Fish carved in mother-of-pearl (above) *and greenstone* (right) *from offering 41. L. 4–6 cm.*

The calpulli

The *calpulli*, the basis of Aztec social organization,[6] was a territorial unit or sector of the city often occupied by people with kinship ties. Generally speaking, each individual belonged to a specific *calpulli* and could work land there. The *calpultin* took turns to provide manpower – perhaps twenty to one hundred men – for communal works. This type of community effort was part of the internal "tribute" that the average citizen had to pay to the state. The same occurred in times of war, when a type of draft was exercised. A certain number of men from the *calpultin* went into the army. The military provided a means of social mobility; outstanding feats in war were the only way to improve one's social status.

The market

The market played an important part in the economy as a means of large-scale redistribution of diverse products. We know that the marketplace at

120

Tlatelolco greatly impressed the Spanish conquerors; thousands of people bartered there, in great harmony and order, for an enormous variety of products.[7]

Different kinds of merchandise had to be sold in designated areas of the market. There were separate stalls for such goods as gold and silver, precious stones, feathers, woven products, and even slaves. Bernal Díaz compared the slave market to the one he knew for blacks taken from Guinea by the Portuguese, except that in Mexico most of the slaves wore bulky wooden collars to prevent them escaping.

Foodstuffs were rich and varied: legumes and herbs were sold in one section, fowl and meat – including dogs – in another. Other produce included salt, cacao, fish, patties made with algae from the lake, fruit, and honey cakes. The Spaniards were unfamiliar with tobacco mixed with liquidambar which was sold in tube-shaped pipes. Paper – made of bark called *amatl* – was sold, as was a wide variety of pottery, flint and obsidian implements, and wood for building material and furniture.

Clothing was of both fine material, mainly cotton, and of lesser quality, of maguey fiber. One area was assigned to skins, either tanned or uncured, from ocelot, puma, otter, jackal, deer, and badger. Leather was tanned with human ordure which was collected in canoes tied up in the canals at the ends of the great plaza.

120 Model of the marketplace at Tlatelolco, which was greatly admired by the Spanish conquerors.

Coinage was not used in Mexico prior to the Spanish conquest. Instead, merchandise was either traded for other goods or was purchased with cacao beans, small copper axes or lengths of cloth. Anyone caught cheating was severely punished and judges sat in a court of justice in the marketplace while officials constantly inspected the merchandise in the different sections.

Crowds increased dramatically on festive days. It is difficult to calculate the number of inhabitants in Tenochtitlan as a whole at the time of the Spanish conquest; as a comparison, it has been suggested that Teotihuacan (0–AD 750) had, conservatively, 100,000 inhabitants at the time of its apogee around AD 500, when the city covered about 20 square kilometers. Tula (AD 900–1150) has been postulated to have had 30,000 to 60,000 inhabitants in a city which covered some 14 square kilometers.[8] Various figures for the population of Tenochtitlan have been proposed. Jacques Soustelle[9] argues that Tenochtitlan-Tlatelolco must have had more than 500,000 inhabitants, excluding the neighboring settlements. Cortés calculated the number of inhabitants of the cities near Tenochtitlan: in Iztapalapa there were 15,000, in Mexicalcingo around 3,000, and in Churubusco from 4,000 to 5,000. In the market of Tlatelolco alone Cortés stated that there were above a thousand souls.[10] It must be remembered that Aztec houses, although only one storey high, could each accommodate up to a dozen persons. In my view Edward Calnek[11] is closer to reality when he states that there must have been between 150,000 and 200,000 inhabitants in the city of Tenochtitlan.

Turning to the lives of the inhabitants of Tenochtitlan, what can the chronicles tell us about attitudes to birth, marriage, and death? The writings of Sahagún give us considerable detail on daily life, which is treated in pictorial form in the Codex Mendoza.

Birth

Sahagún relates that a pregnancy was cause for great joy and that the young girl's parents immediately informed close relatives and the principal families of the town. A feast was held in honor of the event, which was then announced to the guests by an elder; he also advised the young couple and their parents on how they should act on this occasion, and reminded them of the part played by the gods. The deceased were remembered, and it was foreseen that the child might die and "pass like a dream."

In the eighth month of pregnancy the elders gathered again in the house of the parents of the young woman to decide who should serve as midwife.

A sweat bath (*temazcal*) was then heated as part of the preparation for the future mother. To ensure that the child would be healthy, the young woman was advised not to sleep during the day lest the baby be born with a deformed face, not to expose herself to the sun or stay near the fire – in case she should burn the child – and not to carry heavy bundles.

When delivery began, the young mother was bathed in the sweat bath and given a herb drink (*cihuapatli*, or *montanoa tomentosa*) to help induce contractions. If delivery was slow, she was fed a brew made from the tail of the opossum (*tlacuache*) to speed up contractions, and sometimes put into the sweat bath again to be gently massaged. If the child died within the womb, the midwife introduced her hand and cut up the baby's body with an obsidian knife to remove it and save the mother's life. But if the delivery was successful, the midwife cried out with a battle cry, because the birth of a child was thought to be a combat between life and death, and the young woman was a warrior who had taken a captive, the child. Women gave birth in a squatting position, which made the delivery easier; this is illustrated in the Codex Borbonicus 13.

The ceremony to celebrate the birth of a child depended on whether it was a boy or a girl. From the moment the baby was born, its sex determined its destiny. Boys were to become warriors, whereas girls had to stay in the home; so if the child was a boy the umbilical cord was buried on the battlefield, and if a girl, it was buried beneath the hearth.

Both mother and child were then addressed ritualistically by elders whose discourses were called *huehuetlatolli* ("words of the ancients"), the words varying according to their social rank. The mother was praised for her warrior-like conduct while prayers on behalf of the child were said to Chalchiuhtlicue, goddess of water. The soothsayer (*tonalpouhque*) consulted the pictorial calendar to determine the child's fortune, according to the date and hour of delivery. If the day seemed inauspicious a more favorable one was chosen. The ancient ritual-divinatory calendar of 260 days, *Tonalpohualli*, was at times used in a way similar to our modern horoscope. Some days were considered lucky, and others unlucky.

32

The ceremony which Sahagún calls "baptism" was really a ritual naming of the child, carried out by the midwife. Miniature objects, often of amaranth-seed dough, were made: for a boy, a shield, bow and four arrows symbolizing the four quarters of the world, for a girl, spinning and weaving implements and articles of clothing.

The child was cleansed of any impurities by water poured over the head, in honor of Chalchiuhtlicue, so that he or she would grow like the plants. A girl would be placed in her cradle after the bathing ceremony, while a boy was raised to the sun four times, with the miniature weapons of shield, bow, and arrows laid out. In this ceremony dedicated to the newborn, the two major concerns of Aztec society – water (to give life), and weapons (symbolizing warfare) – were both present.

Education and work

Parents advised their children, often with long and flowery speeches, about aspects of life such as social and sexual conduct, and humility. Children's education to the time of marriage has already been outlined in Chapter 2. The school known as *calmecac* was for children of dignitaries, and here they were presented to the god Quetzalcoatl. Boys were trained to take over high offices of the state, civil duties, or as priests or warriors; girls learned to do penance and to serve the gods. Within the *telpochcalli*, the school for children of ordinary citizens, mainly crafts were taught. There is little information about this school, perhaps because Sahagún's informants were mostly of noble class. But French anthropologist Jacques Soustelle writes about this school:

The *telpochcalli* produced ordinary citizens, although this did not prevent some of them from reaching the highest rank, and its pupils had much more freedom and were much less harshly treated than those in the religious school ... the boy who went to the *telpochcalli* had many disagreeable and commonplace tasks, such as the sweeping of the communal house; and he went with the others, in bands to cut wood for the school or to take part in public works – the repairing of ditches and canals and the cultivation of the common land.[12]

Each youth was trained to carry out a certain occupation, and when he had mastered this he could marry, because then he could support his own home and family.

Aztec society was extremely complex and included a wide variety of specialists. Nobles were given high-level positions, ranging from the priesthood to the state administration of Tenochtitlan and areas under Aztec control outside the city. There were also numerous intellectuals, including scribes (*tlacuilos*) producing pictorial manuscripts; artists painting murals or clay vessels; architects; sculptors; musicians, dancers, and poets. All these groups worked to reinforce Aztec religious beliefs. Art was also a propagandistic tool used in the service of the state, symbolically proclaiming to the world the greatness and power of Tenochtitlan and the Aztecs.

Four scenes from the Codex Mendocino

121 (right) *A father punishing his son.*

122 (below) *A mother teaching her daughter how to weave.*

123 (bottom) *A daughter learning how to spin.*

124 (opposite) *Marriage: the bride's "huipil," or loose shift, is knotted to the young man's mantle.*

The large ovals or half-ovals shown above each scene on this page indicate the number of tortillas fed to a child of the age represented, each day. The small circles represent beans.

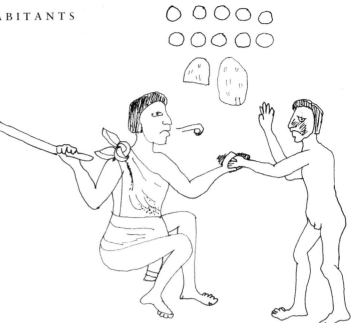

Astronomers played a major role in Aztec society. Because observation of the sun, moon, and stars was intimately related to religion, the priests controlled astronomy, just as they did the calendar and the effect of the seasons on agriculture and other aspects of daily life.

A physician (*ticitl*) could be a man or a woman. Knowledge and use of curative plants was well developed, and all curing practices were preceded by specific rites and ceremonies. There were also a variety of craftsmen, such as metallurgists, stonecutters, ceramists, masons, carpenters, lime-workers, and fishermen.

Marriage

When a young man reached marriageable age he had to request permission from his teachers to leave school, and they were then invited to a banquet organized by his kinsmen, where *mole* (a rich chile and chocolate dish), tamales and cocoa were served. After the feast, the elders among the young man's family placed a fine stone axe before the kinsmen and schoolmasters, symbolizing the respect the youth held for his teachers and at the same time his separation from them.

Another gathering of family and kinsmen took place to choose the young man's wife. A matchmaker (*cihuatlanqui*) was sent to request the girl's hand which, as a formality, was refused two or three times until, at the fourth request, her family responded to the boy's parents. Soothsayers chose a propitious day for the marriage; favorable days were: *Acatl*, "Reed;" *Ozomatli*, "Monkey;" *Cipactli*, "Crocodile;" *Quauhtli*, "Eagle," and *Calli*, "House."

Wedding preparations were elaborate; guests were served exotic food and drink – including *pulque*, the intoxicating beverage made from the century plant, the maguey agave – and were also given reed canes for smoking tobacco. Toward late afternoon the bride was bathed; her arms and legs were adorned with red feathers to beautify them and her face was brightened with pyrites and sometimes with yellow powder. Then she was seated upon a reed mat, where the elders of the youth's family greeted her.

At sunset, the maiden was carried to the groom's home by an old woman from the youth's family who bore her, tied in a mantle, on her back. Gifts were exchanged between the two families, seated before the hearth. The young man's mother gave her daughter-in-law a long loose shift (*huipil*) and a wrap-around skirt (*cueitl*), and the girl's mother reciprocated with a mantle and a breechclout (*maxtlatl*) for her son-in-law. The matchmaker presiding over this ceremony then knotted the bride's *huipil* to the young man's mantle. The mother-in-law washed out the bride's mouth as an act of purification and fed both the girl and man four mouthfuls of tamales and *mole* sauce.

124

The young couple were then isolated for four days and guarded by the old women matchmakers, while the guests continued feasting. On the fourth day the matchmakers removed the reed mat on which the couple had slept, shook it out and returned it to its usual place. Finally, the young man and wife were counseled about their future conduct, the girl by her husband's older women relatives, and the man by the girl's mother.

Old age and illness

The elders were held in great respect, and were asked for advice on many different occasions. No longer active members of the workforce, they were allowed certain privileges, such as being allowed to drink their fill of *pulque* at feasts (whereas the young were severely punished if they got drunk). Many old men became orators and were often requested to speak eloquently during ceremonies. Older women, too, achieved positions of high status, being consulted in matters of medicine, marriage, and as midwives.

Some prehispanic specialists possessed a vast knowledge of medicine. Herbs were of prime importance, as can be seen by the extensive register of medicinal and other useful plants portrayed in the Codex Badianus, a sixteenth-century treatise on New World flora. Physicians included both specialized doctors and midwives as well as healers who used divination to diagnose illness.

Sahagún describes some curers as "evil women" who employed dubious methods for diagnosis and prophesying the outcome of the disease. Among these methods was the casting of maize kernels which, according to their position when they fell, predicted whether the sufferer would be cured or would die. Another method was to throw kernels into a wooden bowl and cover it; when uncovered, the position of the kernels told the diviner of the outcome of the disease. Knots were yet another system of determining the course of an illness; if the knot came undone, the patient would recover, but if it held, his recovery was doubtful. What today are called *limpias*, "cleansing ceremonies," also took place. A *limpia* is usually done with smoke which envelops the patient, in order to drive out evil airs. Alternatively, an egg can be rubbed over the body to absorb the illness which can then be diagnosed by breaking the egg and studying the yolk.

Special techniques were used to treat children. Some healers sucked the chest of a sick child to draw out the illness; others hung him upside down and shook his head from side to side; and some women "attracted" the illness with their breath, thus removing it from the sufferer, or squeezed the child's palate, or pricked him with a blade.

Death and the afterlife

The Aztecs believed that, when a person died, the *teyolía* or inner force went to one of several afterworlds as determined by the manner of death, and not by the individual's conduct in life. The three main afterworlds were known as Mictlan, Tlalocan and the Ichan Tonatiuh Ilhuicac, "House of the sun."

Most people died a natural death and, whether nobles or commoners, men or women, went to Mictlan, "Land of the Dead." Here *125* Mictlantecuhtli and Mictecacihuatl reigned as lord and lady of the realm. *127* Ritual words were directed to the deceased, to assure him that he would no longer suffer the trials of this world and that his long-departed kin would not return to experience the pains they had endured.

A mortuary bundle was then made in which the deceased was placed in a fetal position, bound with cloths and ritual papers. Water was sprinkled on his head, and then the bowl of water and offerings of incense, bundles of pipes, colored thread and clothing were placed with him. A precious stone bead was put in his mouth as a symbol of the soul; if the person had been of high standing, it was made of jade, if he was a commoner, obsidian was used. Finally the mortuary bundle was burned. The ashes were sprinkled with water and were then placed inside a jar and buried within the house, usually under the floor.

As we saw in Chapter 5, a person's soul or *teyolía* had to go through nine stages to return to the place of origin, the womb, symbolized by Mictlan. Just as the female menstrual cycle was arrested for nine

Symbols of death and fertility

125 Plumbate clay dog from offering 44 in the Stage II Temple. Dogs guided the dead on their journey to Mictlan, the "Land of the Dead." Ht 14.5 cm.

126 Clay brazier with the figure of a deity, possibly an agricultural goddess, found in the Stage IVb Temple. Ht 25 cm.

127 (opposite) A vessel with a representation of death, possibly Mictlantecuhtli, "Lord of the Land of the Dead." From offering 17, Stage IV. Ht 16.6 cm.

128 Effigy of Tlaltecuhtli, "Lord of the Earth," in the form of an earth monster. Found north of the Great Temple complex. Ht 50 cm.

successive occasions to allow the fetus to grow, so a mirror image of these phases is perhaps reflected in the journey of the soul. This may explain – as has been suggested above – why the body was arranged in the fetal position for the journey after death.

Small children who died went to the Tonacatecuhtli Ichan, "House of the lord of sustenance," where they were fed by a milk tree.

Tlalocan, "The place of Tlaloc," was a land of eternal spring, where all kinds of fruits and flowers grew in abundance. This green and flowering paradise was presided over by Tlaloc, rain and earth god, and his assistants, the Tlaloques. Destined for Tlalocan were all those who had drowned or had met a death somehow associated with Tlaloc, such as dropsy or being struck by a bolt of lightning, or perhaps being attacked by an aquatic animal. The type of burial was also determined by the manner of death. The deceased were buried, not cremated, but before they were interred they were adorned in a way fitting to be received into the watery paradise. The forehead was colored with a blue substance (the color of water), amaranth seeds were placed on the head and body as a cape, and a wooden staff (perhaps imitating lightning) was put in the hand. Images of hills made of amaranth dough were placed before the body.

Ichan Tonatiuh Ilhuicac, which means literally "Home of the sun in the sky," was a glorious afterworld where warriors who died on the battlefield or as sacrificial victims went after death. These warriors accompanied the sun on his daily journey across the sky. Women who died in childbirth were also considered warriors, since giving birth was seen as a combat and the child, a captive. As we saw in the last chapter, deceased male warriors conducted the sun from where they dwelt in the east to a point at high noon where the women who dwelt in the west received and escorted it on to sunset, repelling any attack with their flashing shields. This western side of the cosmos was the Cihuatlampa, "Reign of women."

Unlike the other two forms of death, where the deceased went to a designated afterworld for all eternity, those killed in war or as sacrificial captives were reborn. Four years after they died they were changed into birds with fine plumage, or beautiful butterflies, flitting from flower to flower and sucking nectar. Thus, their transcendency was assured. This glorious end for the warrior, his privileged afterlife and his return to the world of the living in such a pleasing form, was one of the rewards for those who took up arms in the service of the state.

129 *Aztecs attack the Spaniards in Tenochtitlan. From the Lienzo de Tlaxcala.*

CHAPTER SEVEN

THE DESTRUCTION
OF TENOCHTITLAN

On 13 August 1521, Tlatelolco, last stronghold of the Aztec empire, fell to Hernán Cortés. Tenochtitlan had earlier suffered seventy days of a crippling siege, the climax of which was the capture of Cuauhtemoc, the last *tlatoani*, and the subsequent surrender of the city.

129, 130
131

The Spanish conquest of Tenochtitlan was aided by two factors inherent in Aztec culture. First, the Spaniards encountered a situation of political instability based on economic unrest, which they manipulated to their advantage by gaining Indian allies who were rebelling against the Aztecs. And secondly, the Aztecs' religious beliefs prevented them from defending themselves adequately and fighting to their maximum capacity.

The military conquest

When Cortés reached Mesoamerica in AD 1519 he met with much violent resistance, especially in the lands occupied by the Maya. But in the territory that is today's state of Veracruz, then occupied by the Totonacs who were subject to Tenochtitlan, Cortés learned of the economic and political relationship that existed between the Aztecs and all the tribute-paying peoples on both coasts and in the interior of the country, and detected the hostility against the oppressors. He soon perceived his military potential to consist not only of his few hundred soldiers, but also of Aztec enemies, as well as of the Aztec-conquered towns which were on the point of rebellion. Confident of his success, he was willing to risk his own life as well as the lives of his men by sinking his ships and leading his forces inland to begin the conquest of Mexico.

Thousands of soldiers from different native towns marched with the Spaniards against Tenochtitlan. Both Cortés and Bernal Díaz mention contingents of troops from Tlaxcala (never subdued by the Aztecs),

130 Another scene from the Lienzo de Tlaxcala showing the battle between the Aztecs and the Spanish for control of Tenochtitlan.

Huexotzinco, Chalco, Texcoco, and other allied cities whose forces totaled more than 20,000 men. The Lienzo de Tlaxcala, a pictorial document from the sixteenth century, shows Tlaxcalan soldiers fighting side by side with the Spanish.

The Aztecs practiced what is known as the "flowery war" against other people of the central highlands, mainly the Tlaxcalans. This consisted of, where possible, taking soldiers prisoner rather than killing them, so that they could be sacrificed to the gods. This custom meant that the Aztecs attempted to capture the Spaniards and their Indian allies alive, a policy which put them at a severe disadvantage when the enemy was intent on their eradication. Cortés himself fell prisoner and was being led away when his lieutenant De Olea realized what was happening and, attacking, managed to free his leader. The Europeans understood war as a fight to the death and this attitude must have influenced their Indian allies, who would have followed suit.

The superior military technology of the Spaniards was no doubt also a major contributory factor in their success. Spanish soldiers used metal weapons, whereas indigenous warriors handled arms primarily made of wood with obsidian or flint points or blades. The Spaniards also used the horse in battle, an animal previously unknown to the Aztecs, and built brigantines of war on the lake shores.

Initially the Aztecs viewed Cortés as the god Quetzalcoatl, the prophecy of whose reappearance from the east was fulfilled in the Spaniard's arrival in Veracruz. They soon realized their mistake, however, and tried to repel the conquistadores, first by plying them with gifts and then, when this was unsuccessful, by resorting to battle. The Aztecs knew that the foreigner was an enemy with sophisticated and deadly weapons, but there were also the native allies to face. Motecuhzoma II decided to act cautiously in dealing with these two opponents, an indecisive approach which led to his downfall.

The religious conquest

After the military conquest the Spaniards attempted to change the Aztecs' religious beliefs. Three Christian orders arrived in Mexico: the Franciscans in 1524, originally only twelve in number; the Dominicans in 1526; and the Augustinians in 1533. These religious groups had, in fact, been preceded by friars accompanying Cortés' army – such as Friar Bartolomé Olmedo, who celebrated the first Catholic mass in Mexico. As we saw in the Introduction to this book, the friars set about learning the language, customs, and beliefs of the Indians in order to understand the Aztec mind and use this knowledge in proselytization.

Sahagún, in the prologue to his well-known *General History of the Things of New Spain*, writes:

The physician cannot advisedly administer medicines to the patient without first knowing of which humor or from which source the ailment derives. The preachers and confessors are physicians of the souls for the curing of spiritual ailments. It is good that they have practical knowledge of medicines and the spiritual ailments. Nor is it fitting that the ministers become neglectful of this

131 The final deadly struggle between the Spanish and the Aztecs in Tenochtitlan. From the Lienzo de Tlaxcala.

conversion by saying there are no sins among these people other than orgies, thievery, and lustfulness, because there are many other, much graver sins . . . which are in great need of remedy. The sins of idolatry, idolatrous rituals, idolatrous superstitions, auguries, abuses, and idolatrous ceremonies are not yet completely lost. To preach against these matters, and even to know if they exist, it is needful to know how they practiced them in the times of their idolatry, for, through [our] lack of knowledge of this, they perform many idolatrous things in our presence without our understanding them.[1]

The sixteenth-century friars used various approaches to convert the Indians to Catholicism. They often tried to implant elements of pagan indigenous religious practices into a new Christian context. One method, which utilized the Aztecs' custom of participating in outdoor ceremonies – so common in prehispanic times – was the presentation of plays and farces that lasted for several days and in which the Indians took an active part. This was true theater for the general public in which Catholicism was shown to triumph over paganism, or else the Christians were portrayed victorious over the Moors. These traveling plays became famous; among them were the "Conquest of Rhodes," performed in Mexico City in 1538, and, in 1539, "The Destruction of Jerusalem," enacted in Tlaxcala.[2] At the end of each performance baptism was given to the large number of Indians who had participated as actors or observers.

Another form of evangelization was used by Friar Jacobo de Testera. Basing his ideas on pictorial representations in prehispanic codices, he reproduced a number of Christian prayers in the form of drawings.

The need to communicate this evangelical message to an ever wider audience led the friars to adapt religious architecture to this end. In prehispanic times, religious rites and festivals had been celebrated by large numbers of people in great open spaces; the interior of the temple was reserved only for the use of priests. To rectify this situation, open chapels were constructed. These were built at one side of the church or monastery to take advantage of the large courtyard or atrium in front, where the masses of new converts gathered. This meant that ceremonies were carried out in the great courtyard just as they had been in earlier times.

As part of the ideological struggle, the friars ordered the destruction of prehispanic temples and then used the same stones and manpower to build the first colonial churches and monasteries. The destruction of the old buildings and the construction of the new was so great that a sixteenth-century friar, Toribio de Benavente, better known as Motolinía, compared this with one of the ten plagues of Egypt, writing in his *Memoriales*:

The seventh plague [was] the building of the great city of Mexico. During the first few years more people were occupied [in this] than in the erection of the Temple of Jerusalem in the time of Solomon, because so many people labored in this work, or came bearing [building] material, or supplying food for the Spaniards or for those who were employed in the project, that it was barely possible to move through the streets and highways, although these were very wide. And in this work, some carried the beams, while others fitted them above, and others had the task of demolishing buildings in one place so that some could be built in other places. It is customary in this type of work that the Indians cover their own expenses; they find the materials and pay the stonecutters or quarrymen and the carpenters, and if they do not bring their own food, they fast. They carry the materials on their backs, the beams and large stones are pulled with ropes. And since ingenuity was lacking but there was an abundance of people, a stone or beam that could be hauled by one hundred men was brought by four hundred; this is customary when bringing the materials. Since many do this [work], they go singing and shouting. These shouts hardly ceased night or day, due to the great zeal with which the city was built during those first years. Now it can be seen whether the seventh plague of Egypt agrees with this . . .[3]

132 *The Old World meets the New, AD 1519. Cortés with nobles of the Tlaxcalan state. From the Lienzo de Tlaxcala.*

Motolinía also, however, gives us a glimpse of how the Indians took advantage of any negligence on the part of the Spaniards, to place within the church walls they were building some stone figures of their gods:

So it was seen that they had some [Christian] images within their altars, together with their devils and idols. In other parts the unmistakable image or hidden idol was behind some masonry work, or behind a wall, or within an altar, and that is why they were removed, as many as could be found, and [the Indians] were told that if they wished to have images of God or of the Virgin Mary that they should obey the Church . . .4

In a further attempt to eliminate any vestiges of prehispanic religion, the Spanish conquerors decided to change the central focus of the city. After the destruction of the Great Temple and the original sacred precinct, the Spanish colonial square was built a little farther south, where the present-day Zocalo or central plaza is situated. The area that had been occupied by the Great Temple was divided into lots which were distributed among some of the conquerors. But neither the destruction of the ancient city nor the passage of time have completely wiped out the traces of the site occupied by Tenochtitlan. And so it is that today's city of Mexico stands on those remains, which every once in a while are uncovered to tell us more about the past.

In Tlatelolco, once a separate city but later the northern part of the Aztec capital, a plaque was installed in 1965, which is engraved with the following inscription:

On the 13th of August in 1521,
heroically defended by Cuauhtemoc,
Tlatelolco fell to Hernán Cortés.
This was neither a triumph nor a defeat,
it was a painful birth
of the *mestizo* people
who are the Mexico of today.

133 *The hand and foot of the Coyolxauhqui monolith, found in 1978. Compare half-title page, ill. 14, and color plate III.*

CHRONOLOGICAL TABLE

GLOSSARY OF AZTEC CIVILIZATION

NOTES TO THE TEXT

BIBLIOGRAPHY

LIST OF ILLUSTRATIONS

INDEX

CHRONOLOGICAL TABLE

Ruler's name	Years of reign	Construction Stages and dates of the Great Temple
Earliest rulers unknown	1325 Foundation of Tenochtitlan	Stage I
Acamapichtli Huitzilihuitl Chimalpopoca	1375–1395 1396–1417 1417–1426	Stage II
Itzcoatl	1427–1440	Stage III ("4 Reed," AD 1431)
Motecuhzoma I	1440–1469	Stage IV ("1 Rabbit," AD 1454)
Axayacatl	1469–1481	Stage IVb ("3 House," AD 1469)
Tizoc	1481–1486	Stage V
Ahuitzotl	1486–1502	Stage VI
Motecuhzoma II	1502–1520	Stage VII Arrival of the Spaniards and fall of Tenochtitlan, 13 August 1521
Cuitlahuac	1520	
Cuauhtemoc	1520–1525	

GLOSSARY OF AZTEC CIVILIZATION

Acamapichtli "Handful of Reeds," first Aztec sovereign, AD 1375–1395.

Achitometl Ruler of Colhuacan, father of the girl who was sacrificed and flayed by the Aztecs before they settled at Tenochtitlan.

ahuexotl Willow. *Ahuehuete* (Nahuatl *ahuehuetel: Cypressus distichia; Taxodium mucronatum*) is another tree frequently mentioned in the chronicles, called either a cypress or juniper, according to the source. Both the *ahuehuete* and the *ahuexotl* grow near water or need damp soil. The root of these words is *(a)tl* = water, and *huehue* = old; the *ahuehuete* grows to a venerable old age, one in Oaxaca is said to be more than a thousand years. There are many in Chapultepec in Mexico City, a favorite spot with the Aztec rulers, once rich in springs.

Ahuitzotl "Water Monster," eighth Aztec ruler, AD 1486–1502.

amatl Bark paper, made from the bark of the wild fig tree, *Ficus benjamina. Amatl*, or *amate* as it is called today, was used not only for documents, its surface covered with picture writing, but it also formed part of ritual as banners or as clothing for images of the gods. In ceremonies to the rain gods, *amatl* was sprinkled with liquid rubber, a symbol of water.

Anecuyotl One of Huitzilopochtli's insignia. Also means "destiny."

Atamalaqualiztli "Eating of water tamales," a major ceremony held every eight years in the month of Tepeilhuitl or in Quecholli. It was in honor of vegetation deities, mainly Xochiquetzal, goddess of flowers and grains, and patroness of weavers. For seven days people fasted, eating only maize tamales made with water, similar to unleavened bread. Deity impersonators danced, and some swallowed snakes and frogs in front of the statue of Tlaloc.

atlatl Spear-thrower, used to propel a dart or small spear.

Atlcahualo "Ceasing of water," first month in the 18-month prehispanic year (each month had 20 days), corresponding to February 14–March 5. Also called *Cuahuitlehua*, "Raising of trees," and *Xilomanaliztli*, "Offering of tender young ears of maize." Deities of water and the earth's fertility were honored in this period: Tlaloc, Chalchiuhtlicue, maize goddesses, and Quetzalcoatl. Offerings of corn were given to maize deities in the Great Temple precinct, and children were sacrificed to the Tlaloques, the water gods.

atole Gruel made with a maize base, then sweetened with honey and flavored with fruit or chocolate.

Atzacualco One of the four original *barrios* of Tenochtitlan.

Axayacatl "Water Face," sixth Aztec ruler, AD 1469–1481.

Azcapotzalco "In the anthill," many ants referring to a multitude of people. Capital of the Tepanec state under Tezozomoc.

Aztec "People of Aztlan." See Note 1, Introduction.

Aztlan "White place" or "Place of herons." Mythical original home of the Mexica-Aztecs.

barrio A subdivision in a town, a territorial unit. See *calpulli*.

calmecac School for children of dignitaries where they were taught astronomy, religion, the calendar, history, moral comportment, and other subjects which would permit them to belong to the ruling-administrative class, or the priesthood when they were older. The *calmecac* were attached to temples, and priests were the teachers. Some children of plebeian families attended this school.

calpixqui (pl. *calpixque*) Administrative officials whose major duty was that of collecting taxes and receiving provisions paid as tribute from the different provinces. They were members of the *pipiltin*, or noble class, and were in close communication with the sovereign with regard to the country's welfare, the condition of roads and public buildings, and the maintenance of the palace.

calpullec (pl. *calpulleque*) Head of a *calpulli*, elected for a life term and confirmed by the ruler; he had an advisory council of elders.

calpulli (pl. *calpultin*) Territorial unit, subdivision in a town. Literally *calpulli* "Big house." See Note 1, Chapter 2.

Cemanahuac "In a circle of water," also "In the center of the world."

Centzon Huitznahua "400 Southerners," the innumerable brothers of Huitzilopochtli and Coyolxauhqui; also, the "Innumerable ones of the south," a group of stars.

Centzon Mimixcoa "400" or "Innumerable ones of the north," a group of stars.

chacmool Sculpture of a reclining man with a receptacle on his abdomen, probably for offerings. These sculptures are typical of the Toltec culture but are also found in the Maya area, in the Postclassic period, and are dotted throughout the center, north, and west of Tenochtitlan. A spectacular Aztec chacmool with Tlaloc characteristics is displayed in the Mexica Hall in Mexico's National Museum of Anthropology.

chalchihuitl Jade, green stone. Symbol of that which is precious, symbol of water.

Chalchiuhtlatonac "Glowing Jade," an aspect of Tlaloc, rain-earth deity, consort of Chalchiuhtlicue, water goddess.

Chalchiuhtlicue "She of the Jade Skirt," goddess of ground water such as springs, rivers, lakes, Consort of Tlaloc. The skirt of jades (*chalchihuitl*) symbolizes that which is precious, in this case water.

chia Long-leafed sage (*Genus Salvia*), used mainly for making a refreshing beverage.

Chichimecatl (pl. *Chichimeca*); *Chichimeca-Aztecs* "Dog Lineage," referring to a myth in which a hunter and a dog were the sole survivors after a deluge. The dog was actually a woman and when she shed the dog skin the man burned it; together they started a new line, that of the Chichimec. "Chichimec" also refers to hunters and gatherers, a semi-nomadic people. Chichimecs migrated from Aztlan (thus the Chichimec-Aztecs = these people in a rough state), and settled mainly in Texcoco.

Chicomoztoc "Seven Caves," the legendary birthplace of seven groups, one of them the Aztecs. In myth, Chicomoztoc is often confused with Aztlan, the Aztec homeland, or with Colhuacan, the place of ancestors.

Chiconamictlan Ninth region of the Land of the dead, where the "soul" of the deceased had to cross the Chiconahuapan River on the back of a reddish-orange dog.

Chimalpopoca "Smoking Shield," refers to the sun. The third ruler of Tenochtitlan, AD 1417–1426, was called Chimalpopoca.

chinampa The so-called "floating gardens" in the southern part of Mexico City, made of mud dredged up from the lake bottom and piled onto rafts of branches, thus forming artificial islands. They were/are very fertile, and over the centuries have provided the Mexican capital with vegetables.

Cholula Originally Chololan. City in the present-day state of Puebla, east of Tenochtitlan.

Churubusco Originally Huitzilopochco, "In the house of Huitzilopochtli," now part of Coyoacan in the southern part of Mexico City.

Cihuatlampa "Reign of women," the west, mythical home of women who died in childbirth.

cipactli Crocodile. One of the day signs in the prehispanic calendar.

Cipactonal The first man, husband of Oxomoco, creators of the human race. Seen as an old sorcerer divining with

maize kernels in the Codex Borbonicus 21. Associated with solar and fire aspects and equated with Ometecuhtli, the male half of the primordial creator couple.

Citlalco "Place of stars," the second level in the tiers of the heavens.

Coatepetl, Coatepec "Serpent Hill," site near Tula, Hidalgo, where Huitzilopochtli was miraculously born, fully armed, of Coatlicue, in time to do battle and defeat his 400 brothers the Huitznahua, who, led by their sister Coyolxauhqui, were intent upon killing their mother Coatlicue. It was at Coatepec that Huitzilopochtli decapitated and dismembered Coyolxauhqui. The Great Temple in Tenochtitlan was a symbolic reconstruction of the Coatepetl.

Coatlicue "She of the Serpent Skirt," Mother Goddess, patroness of florists; mother of Huitzilopochtli, the Huitznahua, and Coyolxauhqui. Her great statue is one of the most spectacular pieces in Mexico City's Museum of Anthropology.

Colhuacan, Culhuacan (the "o" and the "u" are interchangeable). "Place of the Culhuas" (a branch of the Toltecs). The word also means "Curved Hill" or "Place of ancestors." The root *coloa* or *culua* means "curved, twisted" and *colli* or *culli*, "grandfather, ancestor." An important city in the southern part of the Valley of Mexico, it is now a section of Mexico City.

Copil Son of Malinalxochitl, one of Huitzilopochtli's sisters, born after his mother's expulsion from the Mexica-Aztec group, based on the fact that she was a sorceress. Copil's heart, taken when he failed to kill his uncle, was thrown into the reeds and rushes and marked the spot where the prickly pear cactus grew and where Tenochtitlan was founded.

Coyoacan "Place of coyotes," in prehispanic times a Tepanec settlement, today a part of Mexico City.

Coyolxauhqui "Bells on her Cheeks," sister of Huitzilopochtli, defeated and dismembered at Coatepec.

Cu Temple, pronounced "coo."

Cuauhtloquetzqui One of Huitzilopochtli's priests, to whom the god communicated in dreams his commands for the Aztecs. It was

Cuauhtloquetzqui who threw Copil's heart into the reeds, which marked the spot where Tenochtitlan was to be founded.

Cuauhxicalli "Eagle vessel," a recipient where hearts of sacrificed victims were deposited.

Cuepopan "Place where flowers blossom," a *calpulli* north of the Great Temple of Tenochtitlan, one of the four original divisions of the city.

Cuicatlicac (*Quauhuitlicac*) One of the 400 Huitznahua, who disagreed with Coyolxauhqui's plan to kill his mother, Coatlicue, and who therefore advised her of the attack so that Huitzilopochtli could be born and defeat the offenders.

Cuicuilco "Place of stone sculpture" or "Place of many colors." Preclassic archaeological site in southern Mexico City.

Cuitlahuac "Water Excrement," "Keeper of the Kingdom," name of the tenth ruler of Tenochtitlan, AD 1520.

Ehecatl-Quetzalcoatl "Wind" "Feathered Serpent," and aspect of Quetzalcoatl. Ehecatl was the wind that swept the roads before the rain.

etzalli; *Etzalcualiztli* Maize and beans eaten together. *Etzalcualiztli*, "Eating of corn with beans," the prehispanic sixth month, corresponding to late May and early June. *Etzalli*, a ritual food, signified the agricultural abundance of the season and was the only time that people were allowed to eat these two foods together. Impersonators of water deities were sacrificed, and ceremonies were held in honor of Tlaloc, Chalchiuhtlicue, and Huixtocihuatl, goddess of salt and salt water.

Huauhquiltamalli; *Huauhquiltamalqualiztli* "Eating of tamales (*huahuquiltamalli*) filled with greens," another name for *Izcalli*, "Growth," eighteenth month of the year (the equivalent of the second half of January through to early February). Xiuhtecuhtli, the Old God of Fire, was honored, a New Fire ceremony was held and a new image of the Fire God was made of amaranth dough. Boys hunted and then tossed the game into the fire as an offering. Xiuhtecuhtli was the patron of rulers so the sovereign played a prominent part in the ceremonies; there was also a great dance of the lords, and special tamales were eaten. Every four years impersonators of Xiuhtecuhtli were sacrificed by fire.

Huehueteotl "Old God," an aspect of Xiuhtecuhtli, Old God of Fire, portrayed as an old man sitting crosslegged, bent over with a brazier on his back or his head. Clay or stone images of Huehueteotl have been found in archaeological excavations in Classic Teotihuacan, in Gulf Coast cultures, and as early as Cuicuilco (Preclassic) in the Valley of Mexico.

Huey Teocalli "Great Temple" in the Nahuatl language.

Huey Tozoztli "Great Vigil," fourth month of 20 days each in the 18-month calendar, corresponding to the second half of April. Ceremonies in honor of the first fruits and of water and maize deities, also Quetzalcoatl, were performed. Important rites were held on the summit of Mount Tlaloc, east of Tenochtitlan, with rich offerings by the Aztec sovereign and rulers of other cities.

huipil Feminine garment, a type of long blouse or shift.

Huitzilihuitl "Hummingbird Feather," second ruler of Tenochtitlan, AD 1396–1417.

Huitzilopochtli "Hummingbird on the Left," possibly referring to the left of the sun, or to the south. Huitzilopochtli was the Mexica-Aztec tutelary deity, associated with war, sun, sovereignty and power. He was the son of Coatlicue and the brother of the Huitznahua and of Coyolxauhqui.

Huitztlampa "Region of thorns," refers to the south.

icpalli Low chair without legs, usually made of wood with a woven mat back. Used by persons of high rank.

Ilhuicatl Xoxouhqui "Blue Sky," appellation given to the statue of Huitzilopochtli in the Great Temple.

Itzcoatl "Obsidian Serpent," fourth Mexica ruler, AD 1427–1440.

Iztapalapa "Across the water," city near Colhuacan, south of Tenochtitlan.

Iztapalnacazcayan Eighth level of the heavens, "Place where the corners are of obsidian blades."

macehual (pl. *macehualtin*) The average person, a commoner.

Malinalxochitl Huitzilopochtli's sorceress sister, mother of Copil.

Maxtla Tepanec ruler of Coyoacan, enemy of Tenochtitlan, who tried to humiliate the Aztecs by inviting them to a banquet and giving them women's clothing to wear: this was interpreted as a declaration of war. Maxtla eventually was defeated by the Aztec sovereign Itzcoatl.

maxtlatl Breechcloth.

Mayahuel Personified maguey or century plant which produces *pulque*, an intoxicating liquor. Although basically associated with this drink which was used principally in ritual, the maguey plant had multiple uses: material for roofing; thread for weaving; and self-sacrifice using the sharp thorns at the ends of the leaves.

mayeque People who lived on and worked the lands of others; tenant farmers. A class lower than that of the *macehualtin*

Mestizo Person of mixed ancestry, Indian and non-Indian.

Mexica-Aztec The branch of the Aztec people who settled in the Valley of Mexico and founded Tenochtitlan. See Note 1, Introduction.

Mexica (pl. *Mexitin*); *Mexican* See Mexica-Aztec, also Note 1, Introduction. "Mexican" is the same as Mexica. Today the people of Mexico are called Mexican.

Michihuauhtli Huauhtli – Seed amaranth (*Amaranthus hypochondriacus*) – was the basic element in the ritual *tzoalli*. *Michihuauhtli* is a type of *huauhtli* whose seeds resemble fish roe (*michin* means "fish" in Nahuatl).

Mictlampa "Place of death," associated with the north.

Mictlantecuhtli "Lord of Michtlan," Land of the dead, god of the last resting place of the deceased.

Mixcoatl "Cloud Serpent," known in some areas as Camaxtli, god of the hunt. Mixcoatl had aspects similar to those of Huitzilopochtli, for example war, but was also twinned to Quetzalcoatl (Morning Star) as the Evening Star. He was the patron of Tlaxcala and Huexotzinco.

Motecuhzoma I Full name, Motecuhzoma Ilhuicamina, "Angry Lord, Archer of the Sky." Fifth Aztec leader who ruled Tenochtitlan AD 1440–1469.

Moyotlan "Place of mosquitoes," section of Tenochtitlan south of the Great Temple, a marshy area, one of the four original divisions of the city.

Nahua; *Nahuatl Nahua*, "He who speaks clearly," a person who spoke Nahuatl, "That which sounds like a bell," according to Friar Alonso de Molina's sixteenth century dictionary. A branch of the Uto-Aztecan linguistic group. See Aztec.

Nanahuatl, Nanahuatzin "He [who is covered] with pustules," the god who threw himself into the fire in Teotihuacan and became transformed into the sun.

Ochpaniztli "Sweeping of the way," the eleventh month, corresponding to the first 20 days of September, in honor of the Mother Goddess. Houses, temples, and roads were swept clean, young warriors fought mock battles, as did midwives, and impersonators of the Mother Goddess and maize deities were decapitated and their flayed skins worn by male dancers. An arrow sacrifice was held, its symbolism said to be fertilization of the earth by the victim's blood. This was basically a harvest festival.

Omecihuatl "Lady Two," companion of Ometecuhtli in Omeyocan; female component of the creator pair. She was also known as Tonacacihuatl, "Lady of Our Sustenance" and Citlalicue, "Her Starry Skirt." Omecihuatl and Ometecuhtli were the primordial parents of the gods, the four aspects of Tezcatlipoca being their first children, and as Oxomoco and Cipactonal they were the primordial parents of humans.

Ometecuhtli "Lord Two," the male half of Omecihuatl, "Divine Two," who dwelt in Omeyocan. Ometecuhtli was also known as Tonacatecuhtli, "Lord of Sustenance." His other names, according to Nicholson (1971), are Citlalatonac, "Glowing Star," Ipalnemoani, "He through whom one Lives," Tloque Nahuaque, "Master of the Near and the Adjacent," and Yoalli Ehecatl, "Night Wind." The last three are also names of Tezcatlipoca in his different guises.

GLOSSARY

Omeyocan "Place of duality," the thirteenth celestial level where the creator pair dwelt.

Oxomoco The first woman, companion of Cipactonal, conceived as an old sorceress, merging with maize-fertility goddesses and with Omecihuatl.

Panquetzaliztli "Raising of the Banners," a feast which took place in the fifteenth month (late November and early December) in honor of Huitzilopochtli. Tezcatlipoca and Yacatecuhtli – the merchant god – were also propitiated. Paper banners decorated homes and fruit trees, the image of Huitzilopochtli was formed of amaranth dough and seeds, many victims were sacrificed to Huitzilopochtli, and merchants also sacrificed slaves. One highlight of the fiesta was a procession led by a priest carrying an image of Painal, Huitzilopochtli's deputy, from the Great Temple to different sectors of the city and back to the center of Tenochtitlan.

pilli (pl. *pipiltin*) Noble, lord, person of high birth. Also means "child."

Preclassic or Formative period 1500 BC–AD 150. In the Valley of Mexico, the Preclassic began a few centuries later than in the Tabasco and Veracruz lowlands.

Quetzalcoatl "Feathered Serpent" or "Precious Twin," god of knowledge and civilization, patron of the *calmecac* school, archetype of priests (Quetzalcoatl gave his name to the high priest). The culture hero and high priest of Tula called Quetzalcoatl, when forced by Tezcatlipoca to leave his city, went to the Gulf Coast of Mexico where he disappeared into the east, thus becoming the Morning Star. In this aspect he was called Tlahuizcalpantecuhtli, and Mixcoatl, his twin, was the Evening Star. As Ehecatl, Quetzalcoatl was the wind.

talud-tablero Architectural profile of a sloping wall (*talud*) combined with a rectangular upright panel (*tablero*), typical of many structures in Teotihuacan. When found elsewhere the *talud-tablero* usually indicates Teotihuacan influence.

Tamoanchan A mythical paradise. Etymology uncertain but according to Sahagún it means "We search for our abode."

techcatl Sacrificial stone over which the victim was bent when the heart was extirpated.

tecpatl First knife used for cutting out the heart of the sacrificial victim. It was also a day sign in the calendar.

tecuhtli (pl. *tetecuhtin*) Man of high rank, one who held an important administrative position; outstanding warrior.

telpochcalli "House of youth," where young men and women of the non-noble class were educated to become average citizens. They were taught by *telpochtlatoque*, "Masters of young men," and by *ichpochtlatoque*, "Mistresses of young girls," who were not religious but lay officials. As Telpochtli, one of his aspects, Tezcatlipoca was the patron of the *telpochcalli*.

Templo Mayor "Great Temple" in Spanish, called thus in Mexico.

Tenochcatl (pl. *Tenochca*) "Person" or "People of Tenochtitlan."

Tenochtitlan "Place of the prickly pear cactus," capital of the Mexica-Aztec empire. In some sources, Tenochtitlan is derived from Tenoch, one of the mythical founders of the city. Tenochtitlan is now Mexico City.

teomama (pl. *teomamaque*) A *teomama*, "god-bearer," was one of the *teomamaque* who carried the image of the god Huitzilopochtli on the migration from Aztlan to the Valley of Mexico.

Teopan "Place of the temple (or god)," one of the four quarters into which Tenochtitlan was originally divided. It lies to the east of the Great Temple.

Teotihuacan "Place where the gods (or rulers) are made," the great Classic metropolis (*c.* 200 BC–AD 750) in the central Mexican highlands, whose influence extended in all directions.

Tepanec, Tecpanec "People of the *tecpan* (palace)" or "People of the *tepan* (rocky land)." A group which settled in Azcapotzalco and Tlacopan (Tacuba). The Aztecs were subservient to the Tepanecs until they overthrew them in AD 1428.

Tepeyacac "Hill of the nose," place north of the Great Temple where in ancient times Tonantzin, "Our Mother," was worshipped. Today the

Shrine of Our Lady of Guadalupe, patroness of Mexico, stands in Tepeyac, as it is now called; it is also called the Villa de Guadalupe.

Tepeyolotl "Heart of the Hill," an aspect of Tezcatlipoca.

tepictoton "Small molded ones," images of hills made of amaranth dough for the thirteenth month, Tepeilhuitl, festivities. The *tepictoton* were also considered to be the Tlaloques, Tlaloc's helpers.

tequihua (pl. *Tequihuaque*) Title given to distinguished warriors or dignitaries who were heads of other administrators.

Tetamazolco Place name, "In (or on) the stone toad."

Tezcatlipoca "Smoking Mirror," supreme god of prehispanic central Mexico; the god of fate, omnipotent, omniscient, associated with rulership. He had more appellations and aspects than any other deity: as a sorcerer he was associated with the night, his were-animal was the jaguar whose spots symbolize stars and who favors darkness. As Yaotl, the warrior-god, he was the enemy, but as Telpochtli he was eternally young. Among his many other aspects Tezcatlipoca was the obsidian knife. And, although he was associated with the moon, his characteristics overlapped with those of Huitzilopochtli, who represented the sun.

tezontle A type of volcanic stone, porous and either gray or reddish in color.

Tezozomoc of Azcapotzalco Tepanec sovereign who ruled for more than half a century, died AD 1426.

Tizapan "Where there is chalk (or chalky water)," a section of Colhuacan, often confused with a neighborhood called Tizapan in San Angel, in the southern part of Mexico City.

Tlacauepan Cuexcotzin Tlacauepan (Tlacahuepan) was an Aztec warrior who was taken prisoner by the Chalcas in a battle; but he had distinguished himself so much by his bravery that the Chalcas offered to spare his life and give him a command of the troops of Chalco. Tlacauepan refused, however, preferring an honorable death to a glorified position among the enemy. Another name for Huitzilopochtli, after whom this Aztec hero was named.

Sahagún also mentions a Tlacahuepan as one of the evil men who destroyed Tula.

Tlacaxipehualiztli "Flaying of Men," also called Coailhuitl, "Serpent Feast Day," second month of the prehispanic year, corresponding to 6–25 March. This was a general festival to the earth and to the planting season. The god Xipe Totec was honored. The gladiatorial sacrifice, *tlahuahuanaliztli*, was practiced, the victims' flayed skins worn for twenty days by men begging food. Children were sacrificed to encourage rain. Leading warriors received gifts and insignia from the ruler. Metal workers, whose patron god was Xipe Totec, also celebrated.

Tlacopan "Where there are poles," Tepanec city, now Tacuba, part of Mexico City.

tlacotli (pl. *Tlacotin*) Slave.

tlacuacuallo "With [fine] food." Huitzilopochtli's mantle, whose embroidered design was that of human bones.

Tlaloc "Earth Lord," god of rain and the earth's fertility, Tlaloc was one of the most highly revered of all prehispanic deities. He was the god who fertilized the earth and made the plants grow. His consort was Chalchiuhtlicue, goddess of ground waters.

Tlaloc Tlamacazqui Priest in the service of the god Tlaloc.

Tlaloque Assistants to Tlaloc, rain-earth god, seen as little Tlalocs. Four Tlaloques were assigned to the four corners of the world where they controlled the different types of rain. They also lived in caves and on mountain tops where they worked with clouds and lightning. The Tepictoton, mountain gods, were considered to be Tlaloques.

Tlamacazque Priests.

Tlapallan "Place of [red] color," name of mythical site; the east.

Tlatelolco "On the Hillock of Sand," sister-city of Tenochtitlan, site of the great market place. Originally *Xaltilalli* in the Nahuatl language, the word comes from *xalli* = earth, *tlatel* = mound or hillock, and *co* = place of, on.

Tlaltilco Preclassic site in the Valley of Mexico.

tlatoani "He who speaks," "He who has the words," that is, the ruler; the supreme ruler if the title is *Huey Tlatoani* (*huey* = big, great).

Tochancalqui "He who lives in our house." Tochancalqui set fire to Huitzilopochtli's magic weapon, the *xiuhcoatl*, at the moment of Huitzilopochtli's birth in Coatepec, thus the god-hero could use it to kill Coyolxauhqui.

Toci "Our Grandmother," one of the names of the Mother Goddess. Toci was patroness of midwives and healers.

Toltecatl (pl. *Tolteca*). Inhabitant of Tollan (Tula). Artist, artisan.

Tonacatecuhtli "Lord of Sustenance," one the creator gods, also called Ometecuhtli.

Tonacatepetl "Hill of sustenance," in mythology, where maize was kept by ants but was discovered by Quetzalcoatl, who transformed himself into an ant in order to steal some grains, which eventually became the basic food for humans.

Tota "Our Father," appellation given to the tree in a rite to Tlaloc during the month of Huey Tozoztli (second half of April), when a child was sacrificed in Lake Texcoco and Tota was "sacrificed" at the same time by being thrust into the water. Tota was also one of the names of the god Xipe Totec.

Tozoztontli "Small Vigil," also called Xochimanaloya, "Flower Offering," third month (26 March–14 April). Water and maize deities were honored, and gardeners and those who worked with flowers made offerings to Coatlicue; planting rites were held in the fields and to the first flowers. Child sacrifices were made to Tlaloc and skins of flayed victims from ceremonies in the previous month, Tlacaxipehualiztli, were ritually buried in an artificial cave in the temple of Xipe Totec.

Toxcatl "Dryness," fifth month (5–24 May), in honor of Tezcatlipoca. Huitzilopochtli and Yacatecuhtli – the merchant god – were also fêted. Young men who had impersonated Tezcatlipoca and Huitzilopochtli for one year were sacrificed. Household implements, together with agricultural tools and instruments for artisans were "purified" by incense, and priests

carrying out these rites were given maize. Images of Huitzilopochtli and other deities were made of amaranth dough, and there were rites to petition rain; ceremonies and dancing were held, the participants decked with popcorn garlands symbolizing the dryness of the season.

Tula Ancient Toltec capital, north of Mexico City, in today's state of Hidalgo.

tzinitzcan Bird of fine plumage, the *Trogonorous mexicanus*.

tzoalli Dough made of ground amaranth seed (*Amaranthus hypochondriacus*), maize, *chía*, honey from the maguey plant, and at times blood. Amaranth was called *huauhtli* by the Aztecs. Figures of some of the deities were made of *tzoalli* in prehispanic festivals.

tzompantli Skull-rack, the fifty-sixth structure mentioned by Sahagún in the ceremonial precinct of Tenochtitlan. Also, the name of a tree, *Erythrina corallodendrum*, whose leaves and bark have medicinal properties.

uictli; *uictli axoquen*; *uitzoctli* Uictli = hoe. *Uitzilin* = hummingbird. *Axoquen* = "bird of white plumage." *Uictli axoquen* = small white bird, probably the image on the hoe handle.

Xipe Totec "Our Lord the Flayed One," patron of gold and silversmiths, also associated with vegetation. During Xipe's feast, Tlacaxipehualiztli, victims were sacrificed and skinned, and their skins then worn by beggars soliciting food. These skins were also thought to have curative properties and mothers took their children to touch them.

xiuatlatl "Turquoise-blue dart-thrower," one of Huitzilopochtli's weapons.

xiuhcoatl "Turquoise-blue Serpent," also referred to as "Fire Serpent," the insignia of Huitzilopochtli; his magic weapon with which he killed Coyolxauhqui and routed the Huitznahua.

Xiuhtecuhtli "Turquoise Lord," "Lord of the Year," the Old God of Fire also known as Ixcozauhqui, "Yellow Face," and Huehueteotl, "Old God." He was conceived as *Teteo innan*, *Teteo inta*, "Mother and Father of the Gods," that is, as an aspect of Ometeotl. Xiuhtecuhtli was the patron of rulers who were usually invested on the day "4 Reed," the god's calendrical sign.

NOTES TO THE TEXT

Abbreviations

INAH Instituto Nacional de Antropología e Historia
UNAM Universidad Nacional Autónoma de México

Introduction

1 Aztecs, Mexicas (Me-SHEE-cas), Mexicans (MEX-i-cans): "Aztecs" refers to the people of Aztlan. This is the overall group of speakers of the Nahuatl language, a branch of Yuto-Aztecan. The Mexica (plural, Mexitin), more commonly referred to as Mexicas, constituted a subgroup; therefore while the Mexica originally were Aztecs, not all Aztecs were Mexica.

2 The chroniclers who wrote about the Aztecs, the Valley of Mexico, and other people and regions, did so for different reasons. Some of them, like Sahagún, Durán, Mendieta, Torquemada, Motolinía, Burgoa, and Clavijero, were members of Religious Orders. Many were either requested by their Orders to write their accounts or they investigated prehispanic and early colonial religion, history, and custom in order to "prove" that the ancient gods were devils, and the people heathens. Some of these men learned the native languages or wrote in the language of the people they studied, among them Molina, Olmos, and Sahagún. Friar Diego Durán, who came to Mexico as a child and grew up speaking Nahuatl, was also able to understand the ancient pictorial codices, as undoubtedly could other colonial scholars. Durán was a member of the Dominican Order, and is considered a secular writer.

Native Mexican writers cited in this book are Hernando Alvarado Tezozomoc, and Chimalpahin. Tezozomoc wrote two chronicles (c. 1598) which are related to the writings of Durán and Tovar, and to the *Crónica X*, which is thought to be a native

document consulted by the above authors for their histories. Domingo Francisco de San Antón Muñón Chimalpahin, born in the latter part of the sixteenth century, wrote (in Nahuatl) eight *Relaciones* about Colhuacan and Central Mexico. Some have been translated into Spanish or French.

At least one sixteenth-century historian, Bernal Díaz del Castillo, wrote his book as an account of his own part in the Spanish conquest and as a plea for what he considered just remuneration from the Crown. Cortés's letters to the king had as their objective not only to inform his sovereign of different aspects of the conquest, but also to elevate his own reputation and secure further honors.

The *Relaciones Geográficas*, mainly written from 1577 to 1648, while others date from the later seventeenth and eighteenth centuries, were answers to a questionnaire compiled on the order of Felipe II of Spain and sent to authorities in New Spain, of which Mexico formed the major part. Their objective was to record the geography, demography, principal settlements, natural resources, religion, customs, language, and other data useful for the control and exploitation of the extensive territories of Middle and South America. These written accounts were accompanied by maps. For information on the RG's (as they are called) see the *Handbook of Middle American Indians, Guide to Ethnohistorical Sources*, Part One, Volume 12, University of Texas Press, Austin 1972, especially pages 183–242 by Howard F. Cline, *The Relaciones Geográficas of the Spanish Indies, 1577–1648*.

3 León y Gama, Antonio de, 1972. This study refers to the discovery of the Aztec sculptures now known as the colossal Coatlicue and the Aztec Calendar Stone (also called the Sun Stone), both in the National Museum of Anthropology in Mexico City.

Chapter 1

1 Ruiz, Sonia Lombardo de. *Desarrollo urbano de Mexico-Tenochtitlan*, México 1973: 120.

2 *See* Introduction, Note 3.

3 Mier, Servando Teresa de. *Memories*, Madrid n.d.

4 Ibid.

5 Humboldt, Alexander von, 1878.

6 Ibid.

7 Batres, Leopoldo, 1902.

Chapter 2

1 A *barrio* is a section of a city in which live a group of people united by family ties and religion. *Barrio* and *calpulli* are virtually synonymous: *barrio* is the Spanish name, *calpulli* (plural, calpultin) is Nahuatl.

2 The name Aztlan means, as Durán states, "The White Place" or "The Place of Herons." Few historians agree on the location of this semi-mythical place of departure of the Aztecs. What does seem to be clear in the chronicles is that it was an island in a lake. Thus, the Aztecs had a background of an aquatic economy, and their promised land, eventually found in the Valley of Mexico, had this same image. Some modern scholars believe the original Aztlan to be in the central part of Mexico, in the Bajio Region, while others identify it with Aztatlan in the present-day state of Nayarit. For reference to these, see Paul Kirchhoff and Wigberto Jiménez Moreno in the bibliography.

3 Chimalpahin, 1965: 65. The Aztecs are called Chichimecs at the beginning of their migration because this word sometimes refers to semi-nomadic, or "rough" and unpolished people, as the Aztecs supposedly were at that time.

4 Tezozomoc, Hernando Alvarado, 1975: 14–15. Chicomoztoc, "Seven Caves," was the mythical place of creation, often confused with Aztlan and/or Colhuacan (or Culhuacan, in Nahuatl o and the u are interchangeable). Some chronicles mention Chicomoztoc as being a short distance beyond Aztlan, while Durán's illustrations show the Aztecs emerging from one of the Seven Caves at the beginning of the migration. In the Codex Boturuni of *Tira de la Peregrinacion*, Aztlan is seen as an island on which there are seven temples, probably representing Chicomoztoc.

5 See Kirchhoff, Paul, et al., 1976.

6 Colhuacan or Culhuacan literally means "Place of the Colhua people" but *coloa* or *culua* in Nahuatl also means "curved, twisted" and *colli* or *culli* means "grandfather," by extension "ancestor." Thus, the glyph for Colhuacan is a curved hill and one of the meanings, perhaps the most accepted, is "Place of Ancestors." This definition fits well with the Mexican's claim that their ruling line descended from the Colhua-Toltecs of Colhuacan in the Valley of Mexico, because their first *tlatoani* (leader) was the son of a princess of Colhuacan.

7 Durán, D., 1951, vol. I: 17.

8 Tezozomoc, Hernando Alvarado, 1975: 24. The *tzinitzcan* bird, of shiny black feathers, is the *Trogonorus mexicanus*.

9 This is a free rendition of the birth of Huitzilopochtli in Sahagún's Book 3, Chapter 1; 1969; vol. I: 271–272.

10 Sahagún, Bernardino de, 1969, vol. I: 272–273.

11 Friar Diego Durán describes the Mexica's find in the *Historia de las Indias de Nueva España*, 2 vols, Editora Nacional, México 1951; vol. I: 37. When the Toltecs, at the end of their migration, reached the *Tlachiualtepec*, a man-made hill or pyramid, in Cholula, they found ". . . the place of dark waters, where the quetzal bird stands, where the bed of water stretches out, where the white quail awakens . . . where the white eagle feeds . . . where blue water flows . . . where white reeds

grow . . . where white rushes grow . . . where white willows stand . . .," *Historia Tolteca-Chichimeca*, Antigua Librería Robredo, Porrúa, México 1979: 79 and plate VIII.

12 Durán, D., 1951, vol. I: 37–38.

13 Durán, D., 1951, vol. I: 37–38.

14 Durán, D., 1951, vol. I: 40.

15 Durán, D., 1951, vol. I: 40.

16 Cortés, Hernan. Letter to the king in *Cartas de Relación de la Conquista de America*, ed. Nueva España, México, n.d.

17 Durán, D., 1951, vol. I: 42.

18 Carrasco, Pedro, 1971: 363–375.

19 Acamapichtli, whose name means "Handful of Reeds," an Acolhua-Toltec noble from Colhuacan, became the ruler of Tenochtitlan in 1372, one year after Tezozomoc ascended the throne of Azcapotzalco, according to Nigel Davies, 1973: 41, 317.

20 Durán, D., 1951, vol. I: 55.

21 Durán, D., 1951, vol. I: 77. *Chía* is a type of sage. A refreshing beverage is made from *chía* seeds, probably sweetened with honey in prehispanic times.

22 Zorita, Alonso de, 1963.

23 Katz, Friedrich, 1966: 94.

24 Carrasco, Pedro, 1978: 43.

25 Katz, F., 1966: 94.

26 *Tequihua* was also a title given to an official at the service of the state.

27 Rojas, Tereasa, 1983: 181–214.

28 Parsons, Jeffrey et al., 1982.

29 West, Robert and Pedro Armillas, 1950: 165–182.

30 Palerm Angel, 1973: Palerm, Angel and Eric Wolf, 1980.

31 Rojas, Teresa, 1985: 129–231.

32 Sahagún, Bernardino de, 1969, vol. I: 225; vol. IV: 336.

33 Sahagún, Bernardino de, 1969, vol. I: 230.

34 *Durán's Book of the Gods and Rites and The Ancient Calendar*, translated and edited by Fernando Horcasitas and Doris Heyden, University of Oklahoma Press, Norman 1971: 430.

Chapter 3

1 Caso, Alfonso, "Los Calendarios Prehispanios." UNAM, Instituto de Investigaciones Historicas, Cultura Nahuatl, *Monografias*, 6, Mexico City.

2 Díaz del Castillo, Bernal, 1943.

3 Sahagún, B. de, 1969 vol. I: 232–242.

4 Ibid

5 Durán, Diego, 1967 vol. II: 82.

6 Ibid, vol. II: 81.

7 All these dates are subject to revision.

8 Sahagún, B. de, 1969 vol. I: 232.

Chapter 4

1 Batres, Leopoldo, in Matos M. (ed.), 1979: 61–90. Batres found some Maya-style greenstone pieces during his excavations in the Great Temple area. However these may have been heirlooms or chance local finds by the Mexicas, rather than specimens of tribute payment.

2 Gibson, Charles, 1971: 376–394. On page 381 of this volume there is a map of imperial expansion. The later rulers Ahuitzotl and Motecuhzoma II also made considerable advances in Guerrero, but their levels of the Great Temple, Stages VI and VII respectively, were more scantily represented by offerings, perhaps due to severe damage incurred at the time of the Spanish Conquest.

3 Nicholson, H. B., and Eloise Quiñones Keber, 1983: 87–89.

4 Nagao, Debra. "The planting of sustenance: Symbolism of the two-horned god in offerings from the Templo Mayor," *Res* 10: 5–27, Autumn, 1985.

5 Nicholson, H. B., 1971: 413.

6 Sahagún, when describing the ceremonies of the first month of the year, *Atl caualo* or *Quauitl eua*, says: "In this month they slew many children; they sacrificed them in many places upon the mountain tops, tearing them from their hearts, in honor of the gods of water, so that these might give them water or rain" (1982: 1).

7 López Austin, Alfredo, 1979: 133–153.

8 González, Carlos and Bertina Olmedo, 1986: 255–266.

9 Jeffrey Wilkerson, personal communication.

10 Nicholson, H. B. and Eloise Quiñones Keber, 1983: 95.

11 Gibson, 1971.

12 Heyden, Doris, 1984: 23–32.

13 Striking examples of such sites include Chalcatzingo in Morelos (see Grove, David C., *Chalcatzingo. Excavations on the Olmec Frontier*, Thames and Hudson, London and New York 1984). For a site in Guerrero, see Guadalupe Martínez Donjuan, "Teopantecuanitlan," in Vegasosa, Constanza and Roberto Servantes Delgado (eds.), *Primer Coloquio de Arqueología y Etnohistoria del Estado de Guerrero*, INAH, Gobierno del Estado de Guerrero, México, 1986: 55–80.

14 Batres, Leopoldo *op cit*. Batres illustrates a very large lapidary stone figure similar to those found recently at Teotihuacan. See Jarquin Pacheco, Ana María and Enrique Martínez Vargas, "Les Excavaciones en el Conjunto 1-D," in *Memoria del Proyecto Arqueológico Teotihuacan 80–82*, coordinated by Rubén Cabrera Castro, Ignacio Rodríguez G. and Noel Morelos G., INAH, México, 1982: 89–126. Also Jarquin Pacheco, Ana María and Enrique Martínez Vargas, "Una escultura tardía teotihuacana," in *Teotihuacan 80–82, Primeros Resultados*, coordinated by Rubén Cabrera Castro, Ignacio Rodríguez G. and Noel Morelos G., INAH, México, 1982: 121–127.

15 *Relación de San Juan Teotihuacan 1580*, in Francisco del Paso y Troncoso (ed.), *Papeles de Nueva España*, Madrid, Spain, 1905, vol. VI: 219–226. There is a volume for each *Relación*; this volume is a sixteenth-century questionnaire.

16 Polaco, Oscar, in preparation.

17 Díaz-Pardo, Edmundo, in preparation.

18 Alvarez, Ticul, in preparation.

19 Sahagún, Bernardino de 1969, *op. cit*. Book 2: 194–198.

20 Many day signs in the Aztec calendar were represented by animals, such as the serpent, rabbit, lizard, deer, dog, monkey, jaguar, eagle, vulture, and *cipactli*. Birds were associated with the world directions while other animals had even more specific meanings, for example the dog which guided the deceased to the world of the dead.

21 See also Nagao, Debra, 1985.

22 Diego Durán describes this statue of Huitzilopochtli as "a dough image made of *tzoalli* dough, which is made of amaranth seeds and maize kneaded with honey." See *Book of the Gods and Rites and the Ancient Calendar*, translated from Spanish into English by F. Horcasitas and D. Heyden, University of Oklahoma Press, Norman 1971: 80; also Note 9 on page 80.

23 Durán, Diego, 1967 vol. II: 228.

Chapter 5

1 Sahagún, Bernardino de *op. cit.*, 1969, vol. II: 187.

2 Codex Vaticanus A 3738, in Lord Kingsborough, *Antigüedades de México*, vol. III.

3 Ibid.

4 López Austin, Alfredo, 1980.

5 Codex Vaticanus A 3738, in Lord Kingsborough, *Antigüedades de México*, vol. III.

6 Sahagún, Bernardino de *op. cit.*, 1969, vol. I: 295.

7 Nowotny, Karl "Tlacuilolli," in the series *Monumenta Americana*, Berlin, 1961, vol. III.

8 González Torres, Yólotl, 1975.

9 *Historia Tolteca Chichimeca* (anonymous author), ed. Kirchhoff, Paul, 1976: 163.

10 Ibid.

11 Heyden, Doris, 1981: 1–40.

12 Durán, Diego, 1967, vol. II: 343.

13 Eliade, Mircea, 1979: 334.

14 Ibid.: 337.

15 Del Paso y Troncoso, Francisco, 1898; León Portilla, Miguel, 1978. These dates refer to excavations.

16 It would seem from descriptions in chronicles that the statue of Coatlicue or Toci, Mother Goddess, also stood at the summit of the Great Temple.

17 The quartering and decapitation of the body are also related to the phases of the moon, which in turn are associated with women.

18 Sahagún, Bernardino de *op. cit.*, 1969, vol. I.

19 Ibid. The name of the mantle, *tlacuacallo*, perhaps refers to anthropophagy, that is, the eating of the flesh of the sacrificed victims, inasmuch as *tlacuacallo* means "*con manjares*," "with victuals;" by extension, "covered with edibles."

20 Durán, 1967, vol. I: 146.

21 Codex Azcatitlan. As has been mentioned, the appearance of the fire-serpent descending from the temple during the Panquetzaliztli festival is perhaps related to this symbolism.

22 Durán, 1967, vol. I: 82.

23 Códice Chimalpopoca, 1975: 121.

Chapter 6

1 Díaz del Castillo, Bernal, 1943.

2 Ibid.

3 Cortés, Hernán. Letter to the king in *Cartas de Relación de la Conquista de América*, ed. Nueva España, n.d., México.

4 Ibid.

5 Díaz del Castillo, Bernal, 1943.

6 See Chapter 2, Note 1.

7 Díaz del Castillo, Bernal, 1943.

8 See *Tula* by Richard Diehl, in this series.

9 Soustelle, Jacques, 1972.

10 Cortés, Hernán *op. cit*.

11 Calnek, Edward, 1970.

12 Soustelle, Jacques, 1964: 175–176.

Chapter 7

1 Sahagún, Bernardino de, 1982: 45–46.

2 Matos Moctezuma, Eduardo, 1981.

3 Benavente, Toribio de (Motolinía). *Memoriales*, 1971.

4 Ibid.

BIBLIOGRAPHY

Abbreviations

INAH Instituto Nacional de Antropología e Historia
UNAM Universidad Nacional Autónoma de México
SEP Secretaría de Educación Pública

ALVAREZ, Ticul. In preparation. "Restos de vertebrados terrestres en la ofrenda 7," in Matos, M. (ed.) *El Templo Major: excavaciones y estudios*, INAH, México.

BATRES, Leopoldo 1979 "Exploraciones arqueologicas en la calle de las Escalerillas," in Matos, M. (ed.) *Trabajos Arqueologicos en el Centro de la Cuidad de Mexico*, INAH, México.

BENAVENTE, Friar Toribio de (Motolinía) 1971 *Memoriales*, UNAM, México.

CALNEK, Edward 1970 "The Internal Structure of Tenochtitlan," in Wolf, E. (ed.) *The Valley of Mexico. Studies in Pre-Hispanic Ecology and Society*: 287–302. A School of American Research Book, University of New Mexico Press, Albuquerque.

CARRASCO, Pedro 1971 "Social Organization of Ancient Mexico," in Wauchope Robert, Gordon Ekholm and Ignacio Bernal (eds.) *Handbook of Middle American Indians, Archaeology of Northern Mesoamerica*, Part One, Vol. 10: 349–375, University of Texas Press, Austin.

—1978 "La economía del México prehispánico," in *Economía Política e Ideología en el México Prehispánico*: 43, Nueva Imagen (ed.), México.

CHIMALPAHIN, Domingo de San Anton 1965 *Relaciones de Chalco-Amaquemecan*, translated from the Nahuatl by Rendón, Silvia. Fondo de Cultura Económica, México.

CODEX AZCATITLAN, commentary by Barlow, Robert 1949 *Journal de la Société des Américanistes*, Nouvelle Série, Tome XXXVIII: 101–135, plus 29 plates (separate), Musée de L'Homme, Paris.

CODEX BORBONICUS, commentary by Nowotny, Karl Anton 1974 *Códices Selecti*, Vol. XLIV, Akademische Druck-u. Verlagsanstalt, Graz, Austria.

CODEX BOTURINI, or "Tira de la Peregrinación" 1975 Secretaría de Educación Pública, México. No text or commentary.

"CODEX VATICANUS-A Latino 3738 (Códice Ríos)," 1964 in *Antigüedades de México de Lord Kingsborough*: 7–313, Secretaría de Crédito y Hacienda Pública, México.

CÓDICE CHIMALPOPOCA, Anales de Cuauhtitlan y Leyenda de los Soles, 1975, translated from the Nahuatl by Velázquez, Primo Feliciano, Instituto de Investigaciones Históricas, UNAM, México, 2nd edition.

COE, Michael D. 1984 *Mexico*, third edition, Thames and Hudson, London and New York.

CORTES, Hernán n.d. *Cartas de Relación de la Conquista de América*, Nueva España (ed.), México.

DAVIES, Nigel 1973 *The Aztecs. A History*, Macmillan, New York and London.

DIAZ DEL CASTILLO, Bernal 1943 *Historia verdadera de la conquista de la Nueva España*, Nuevo Mundo (ed.), México.

DIAZ-PARDO, Edmundo. In preparation. "Restos de peces procedentes de la ofrenda 7," in Matos, M. (ed.) INAH, México.

DIEHL, Richard 1983 *Tula*, Thames & Hudson, London and New York.

DURAN, Friar Diego 1951 *Historia de las Indias de Nueva España*, 2 vols, Editora Nacional, México.
—1967 *Historia de las Indias de Nueva España e Islas de la Tierra Firme*, Angel María Garibay K. (ed.) 2 vols, Editorial Porrúa, México.
—1971 *Book of the Gods and Rites and the Ancient Calendar*, translated from Spanish into English by Horcasitas, F. and Heyden, D., University of Oklahoma Press, Norman.

ELIADE, Mircea 1979 *Tratado de historia de las religiones*, Biblioteca Era, México.

GIBSON, Charles 1971 "Structure of the Aztec Empire," in Wauchope Robert, Gordon Ekholm, and Ignacio Bernal (eds.) *Handbook of Middle American Indians* Part One, vol. 10: 376–394, University of Texas Press, Austin.

GONZALEZ, Carlos and Bertina Olmedo 1986 "Piezas antropomorphas del estilo Mezcala en el Templo Mayor," in Vega Sosa, Constanza and Roberto Cervantes Delgado (eds.) *Primer Coloquio de Arqueología y Etnohistoria del Estado de Guerrero*: 255–266, INAH, Gobierno del Estado de Guerrero, México.

GONZALEZ TORRES, Yólotl 1975 *El culto a los astros entre los mexicas*, SEP Setentas, México

GROVE, David C. 1984 *Chalcatzingo, Excavations on the Olmec Frontier*, Thames and Hudson, London and New York.

HEYDEN, Doris 1976 "El simbolismo de las plumas rojas en el ritual prehispanico," *Boletín INAH*, Época II, No. 18: 15–22, México.
—1981 "Caves, Gods and Myths: world-view and planning in Teotihuacan," in Benson, Elizabeth P. (ed.) *Mesoamerican sites and world views*: 1–40, Dumbarton Oaks, Washington DC.
—1984 "Las anteojeras serpentinas de Tlaloc," *Estudios de Cultura Nahuatl* 17: 23–32. Instituto de Investigaciones Históricas, UNAM, México.

HUMBOLDT, Alexander von 1878 *Vistas de las cordilleras y monumentos de los pueblos indígenas*, América, Madrid.

KATZ, Friedrich 1966 *Situación Social y Económica de los Aztecas*, UNAM, México.

KIRCHHOFF, Paul 1976 *Historia Tolteca-Chichimeca*, CISINAH (ed.), México.

LEON Y GAMA, Antonio 1792 *Historical and chronological description of the two stones found in the main square of Mexico on the occasion of the paving of this square*, México. (In Spanish.)

LEON PORTILLA, Miguel 1978 *El Templo Mayor de Tenochtitlan, su espacio y tiempos sagrados*, INAH, México.

LOMBARDO DE RUIZ, Sonia 1973 *Desarrollo urbano de México-Tenochtitlan*, México.

LOPEZ AUSTIN, Alfredo 1979 "Iconografía Mexica. El monolito verde del Templo Mayor." in *Anales de Antropología* 16: 133–153, Instituto de Investigaciones Antropológicas, UNAM, México.
—1980 *Cuerpo humano e ideología*, vol. II, University of Mexico, México.

MACNEISH, Richard S. 1972 *The Prehistory of the Valley of Tehuacan*, University of Texas Press, Austin.

MARTINEZ DONJUAN, Guadalupe 1986 "Teopantecuanitlan," in Vega Sosa, Constanza and Roberto Cervantes Delgado (eds.) *Primer Coloquio de Arqueología y Etnohistoria del Estado de Guerrero*: 55–80, INAH, Gobierno del Estado de Guerrero, México.

MATOS MOCTEZUMA, Eduardo 1980 "El Templo Mayor de Tenochtitlan," in *Antropología Americana* No. 1, México.
—1981 *Estudios de Cultura Popular*, Instituto Nacional Indigenista, México.

NAGAO, Debra 1985, Autumn "The planting of sustenance: Symbolism of the two-horned god in offerings from the Templo Mayor," in *Res* 10: 5–27.
—1985 *Mexica Buried Offerings, a Historical and Contextual Analysis*, BAR International Series 235, Oxford.

NICHOLSON, Henry B. 1971 "Religion in Pre-Hispanic Central Mexico," in Wauchope Robert, Gordon Erkholm, and Ignacio Bernal (eds.) *Handbook of Middle American Indians*, Part One,

vol. 10: 395–446, University of Texas Press, Austin.

NICHOLSON, H. B. and Eloise Quiñones Keber 1983 *Art of Aztec Mexico. Treasures of Tenochtitlan*, National Gallery of Art, Washington DC.

NOMBRES GEOGRAFICOS DE MEXICO 1979, compiled by César Macazaga Ordoño, Editorial Cosmos, México.

NOWOTNY, Karl 1961 "Tlacuilolli," *Monumenta Americana* vol. III, Berlin.

PACHECO, Jarquin, Ana María and Enrique Martínez Vargas 1982 "Las excavaciones en el Conjunto 1-D," in Ruben Cabresa Castro, Ignacio Rodríguez, and Noel Morelos (eds.) *Memoria del Proyecto Arqueológico Teotihuacan 80–82*, vol. 1: 89–126, INAH, México.
—1982 "Una escultura tardía teotihuacana," in Ruben Cabresa Castro, Ignacio Rodríguez, and Noel Morelos (eds.) *Teotihuacan 80–82, Primeros Resultados*, vol. 1: 121–128, INAH, México.

PALERM, Angel 1973 *Obras Hidráulicas prehispanicas*, SEP-INAH, México.

PALERM, Angel and Eric Wolf 1980 *Agricultura y Civilización de Mesoamérica*, SEP-Setentas-Diana, México.

PARSONS, Jeffrey, et. al. 1982 *Prehispanic settlement Pattern in the Southern Valley of Mexico. The Chalco-Xochimilco Region*, Memoirs of the Museum of Anthropology, No. 14, University of Michigan, Ann Arbor.

PASO Y TRONCOSO DEL, Francisco 1982 *Descripción, historia y exposición del Códice Borbónico, 1898*, INAH, México.

PEÑAFIEL, Antonio 1910 *Destrucción del Templo de México Antiguo y los monumentos encontrados en la ciudad en las excavaciones de 1897 y 1902*, México.

POLACO, Oscar. In preparation. "Los invertebrados de la ofrenda 7," *El Templo Mayor: excavaciones y estudios*, in Matos, M. (ed.) INAH, México.

ROJAS, Teresa 1983 "Evolución histórica del repertorio de plantas cultivadas en las Chinampas de la Cuenca de México," in Rojas, T. (ed.) *La Agricultura chinampera. Compilación histórica*: 181–214, Universidad Autónoma Chapingo, México.
—1985 "La tecnología mesoamericana en el siglo XVI," in Rojas, T. and W. T. Sandars (eds.), *Historia de la agricultura. Epoca prehispánica-siglo XVI*: 129–231, INAH, Colección Biblioteca del INAH.

SAHAGUN, Friar Bernardino de 1969 *Historia General de las Cosas de Nueva España*, Angel María Garibay K. (ed.), 4 vols, Porrúa, México, 2nd edition.
—1982 *Florentine Codex. General History of the Things of New Spain. Introductions and Indices*, translated from the Nahuatl by Anderson, Arthur J. O. and Charles E. Dibble. Preface by Miguel León-Portilla. Translation of the Prologue from the Spanish by Charles E. Dibble. The School of American Research and The University of Utah, Monographs of the School of American Research, Santa Fe, New Mexico.

SOUSTELLE, Jacques 1964 *Daily Life of the Aztecs on the eve of the Spanish conquest*, Penguin Books, Harmondsworth, Middlesex, England.
—1972 *La vida cotidiana de los Aztecas*, Fondo de Cultura Económica, México.

TERESA DE MIER, Servando n.d. *Memorias*, Madrid.

TEZOZOMOC, Hernando Alvarado 1975 *Crónica Mexicayotl*, México.

WEAVER, Muriel Porter 1981 *The Aztecs, Maya, and Their Predecessors*: 164–172, Academic Press, London and New York.

WEST, Robert and Pedro Armillas 1950 "Las Chinampas de México, poesía y realidad de los jardines flotantes," in *Cuadernos Americanos*, No. 50: 165–182, México.

ZORITA DE, Alonso 1963 *Breve y Sumaria Relación de los Señores de la Nueva España*, UNAM, México.

LIST OF ILLUSTRATIONS

The majority of the photographs are by Salvador Guilliem and are courtesy of the Great Temple Project.

INDEX